NOVELTY CAKES

HAMLYN

Published by The Hamlyn Publishing Group Limited
part of Reed International Books,
Michelin House, 81 Fulham Road, London SW3 6RB

Reprinted 1990

Taken from **Cakes and Cake Decorating** by Rosemary
Wadey and Pat Lock, © 1982, 1985 Hennerwood
Publications Limited, and **Decorative Cakes** by
Rosemary Wadey and Janice Murfitt © 1986 Hennerwood
Publications Limited

Photography by Peter Myers, Vernon Morgan and Clive
Streeter, Artwork by Eugene Fleury

The publishers would like to thank G.F. Smith & Son,
London, Ltd. for permission to use their Parch Marque
papers as background colours for many of the pages in this
book.

ISBN 0 600 55762 6

Typeset in Bembo by Vision Typesetting, Manchester
Produced by Mandarin Offset
Printed and bound in Hong Kong

Contents

Introduction

The first essential step in all cake decorating is to be able to make a good basic cake, whether a simple quick mix or a more elaborate fruit cake. After all, if you are going to spend a lot of time decorating a cake to make it look splendid, then the base should be really good to eat as well. So the first chapter in this book includes all the basic cake recipes that are used in making the novelty cakes, before giving recipes for the various icings which cover and decorate the cakes.

In the chapters which follow, a variety of recipes has been used to produce the different shaped cakes, with the basic Quick Mix Cake, flavoured and coloured, as the basis for many of them. It is baked in a variety of tins and moulds with the minimum amount of trimming needed to obtain the right shape. Whisked sponge mixtures are also trimmed into different shaped cakes, and Swiss rolls are rolled and shaped in unusual ways. Soft cakes should always be made a few days before they are required, to make cutting and shaping them easier.

Butter icings and moulding pastes are the basic coverings for cakes which can be made in advance. Fondant moulding paste is best used at room temperature; use a generous sifting of icing sugar when rolling it out, and always make sure the icing moves freely on the surface during rolling. When moulding or shaping the paste, use clean hands dipped into cornflour. This helps produce a smooth, glossy surface on a flat-iced cake, and prevents sticking when moulding the icing into flowers, animals or trees. Moulded items should be made in parts and left almost to set before being assembled. Use egg white to stick the pieces together.

To achieve a smooth surface on butter icing, use a small palette knife dipped in hot water to prevent it sticking to the surface.

Always use non-stick silicone paper (or baking parchment) to line baking trays before cooking the biscuit dough cut-outs, to ensure the shapes lift off easily and cleanly.

Remember it is important, especially before starting a complicated decoration, to read right through the instructions carefully, then follow them step-by-step. In this way you will avoid finding yourself turning pages with sticky fingers to discover that you are lacking ingredients, short of icing or in need of another piece of equipment to complete the decoration!

The ingenious cake designs and decorations, from the children's novelty cakes and the cakes for special occasions, to the festive cakes for Christmas and the small cakes, are a visual delight and a pleasure to create and eat.

A few simple rules to follow for success

- All spoon measures are level.

- All eggs are size 2 unless otherwise stated.

- Metric and imperial measures have been calculated separately. Use one set of measures only as they are not exact equivalents.

- Cooking times may vary slightly depending on the individual oven. Dishes should be placed in the centre of the oven unless otherwise specified.

- Always preheat the oven to the specified temperature.

Basic Recipes

LINING CAKE TINS

If using special non-stick tins, follow the manufacturer's instructions. With all other tins it is necessary either to grease and flour, or grease and line with greaseproof paper and grease again. Use oil, melted lard or melted margarine for greasing. If you wish to use non-stick silicone paper, there is no need to grease the paper.

Base lining a round or square tin

This method prevents the cake bottom falling out or sticking and is used for sponge and sandwich mixtures and lightly fruited cakes, but not for rich cakes.
1. Cut a single piece of greaseproof paper to fit the bottom of the tin.
2. First grease the inside of the tin completely, then position the paper in the base and grease.

To line or double line a deep round tin

For rich mixtures which require long cooking you should use double thickness of greaseproof paper and line both the sides and base of the tin. With the richer fruit cakes tie two or three thicknesses of brown paper or newspaper round the outside of the tin as an added protection against overcooking the outside of the cake. For less rich mixtures follow the instructions below, using only single thickness greaseproof paper.
1. Cut one or two strips of double greaseproof long enough to reach round the outside of the tin with enough to overlap, and wide enough to come 2.5 cm/1 in above the rim of the tin. Fold the bottom edge up about 2 cm/¾ in and crease it firmly. Open out and make slanting cuts into the folded strip at 2 cm/¾ in intervals.
2. Place the tin on a double thickness of greaseproof paper and draw round the base, then cut it out a little inside the line.
3. Grease the inside of the tin, place one paper circle in the base and grease just round the edge of the paper.
4. Place the long strips in the tin, pressing them against the sides with the cut edges spread over the base. Grease all over the side paper.
5. Finally position the second circle in the base and grease again.

To double line a deep square or rectangular tin

Follow the instructions for the deep round tin but make folds into the corners of the long strips.

To line a shallow rectangular tin

For Swiss rolls and similar cakes it is always wise to line and grease for easy removal.
1. Cut a piece of greaseproof about 7.5 cm/3 in larger than the tin (and larger still if the sides of the tin are deeper than 2.5 cm/1 in).
2. Place the tin on the paper and make a cut from the corners of the paper to the corners of the tin.
3. Grease inside the tin, put in the paper so that it fits neatly, overlapping the paper at the corners to give sharp angles, and grease again.

To line a loaf tin

Use the same method as for lining a shallow rectangular tin but cut the paper at least 15 cm/6 in larger than the top of the tin. Grease the tin, position the paper, fitting the corners neatly, and grease again.

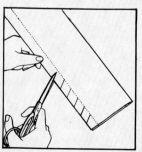
For a round tin, make slanting cuts in the paper

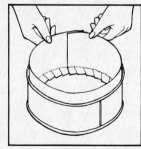
Insert strip

For a rectangular tin, make a cut from the corners

Insert to fit neatly

MADEIRA CAKE

Madeira cake can be covered with marzipan and royal or other icing. The lemon rind and juice may be replaced with orange.

Line and grease a tin, following the instructions on page 5. Cream the butter and sugar together until light and fluffy, and very pale in colour. Beat in the eggs one at a time, following each with a spoonful of flour.

Sift the remaining flours together and fold into the creamed mixture, followed by the lemon rind and juice. Spoon the mixture into the prepared tin and level the top.

Bake in a moderate oven (160 C, 325 F, gas 3) for the time suggested in the chart, or until well risen, firm to the touch and golden brown. Cool in the tin for 5–10 minutes, then turn on to a wire rack to cool and remove the lining paper.

Madeira cake ingredients

CAKE SIZES	15 cm/6 in round or square tin	18 cm/7 in round tin	★18 cm/7 in round tin 900 g/2 lb loaf tin	18 cm/7 in square tin	20 cm/8 in round tin	★20 cm/8 in round tin	20 cm/8 in square tin
butter	100 g/4 oz	100 g/4 oz	175 g/6 oz	175 g/6 oz	175 g/6 oz	225 g/8 oz	225 g/8 oz
caster sugar	100 g/4 oz	100 g/4 oz	175 g/6 oz	175 g/6 oz	175 g/6 oz	225 g/8 oz	225 g/8 oz
eggs (sizes 1,2)	2	2	3	3	3	4	4
self-raising flour	100 g/4 oz	100 g/4 oz	175 g/6 oz	175 g/6 oz	175 g/6 oz	225 g/8 oz	225 g/8 oz
plain flour	50 g/2 oz	50 g/2 oz	75 g/3 oz	75 g/3 oz	75 g/3 oz	100 g/4 oz	100 g/4 oz
grated lemon rind	½–1 lemon	½–1 lemon	1 lemon	1 lemon	1 lemon	1½ lemons	1½ lemons
lemon juice	2 teaspoons	2 teaspoons	1 tablespoon	1 tablespoon	1 tablespoon	4 teaspoons	4 teaspoons
Approx cooking time	*1 hour*	*50 minutes*	*1¼ hours*	*1 hour 5–10 minutes*	*1 hour*	*1 hour 20–25 minutes*	*1 hour 15–20 minutes*

CAKE SIZES	23 cm/9 in round tin	28 × 18 × 4 cm/ 11 × 7 × 1½ in slab cake	★23 cm/9 in round tin	23 cm/9 in square tin	25 cm/10 in round tin	30 × 25 × 5 cm/ 12 × 10 × 2 in slab cake
butter	225 g/8 oz	225 g/8 oz	275 g/10 oz	275 g/10 oz	275 g/10 oz	275 g/10 oz
caster sugar	225 g/8 oz	225 g/8 oz	275 g/10 oz	275 g/10 oz	275 g/10 oz	275 g/10 oz
eggs (sizes 1, 2)	4	4	5	5	5	5
self-raising flour	225 g/8 oz	225 g/8 oz	275 g/10 oz	275 g/10 oz	275 g/10 oz	275 g/10 oz
plain flour	100 g/4 oz	100 g/4 oz	150 g/5 oz	150 g/5 oz	150 g/5 oz	150 g/5 oz
grated lemon rind	1½ lemons	1½ lemons	2 lemons	2 lemons	2 lemons	2 lemons
lemon juice	4 teaspoons	4 teaspoons	2 tablespoons	2 tablespoons	2 tablespoons	2 tablespoons
Approx cooking time	*1 hour 10 minutes*	*1–1¼ hours*	*1 hour 30–40 minutes*	*1 hour 25–30 minutes*	*1 hour 20 minutes*	*1 hour 15–20 minutes*

★These quantities make a deeper cake

VICTORIA SPONGE CAKE

175 g/6 oz caster sugar
175 g/6 oz butter or soft margarine
3 eggs
175 g/6 oz self-raising flour, sifted
1 tablespoon cold water

Cream together the sugar and butter or margarine until light and fluffy and pale in colour. Beat in the eggs one at a time, following each addition with a little of the flour. Using a metal spoon, fold in the remaining flour alternately with the water.

Divide the mixture between two greased and floured 20-cm/8-in round sandwich tins, or fill a 28 × 18 × 4-cm/11 × 7 × 1½-in rectangular cake tin. Level the surface and bake in a moderately hot oven (190 C, 375 F, gas 5) for 20–25 minutes, or until well risen and firm to the touch. Turn out on to a wire rack to cool.

Variations

Chocolate Victoria Sponge Cake
Replace 25 g/1 oz of the flour with 25 g/1 oz sifted cocoa powder. Add with the remaining flour.

Coffee Victoria Sponge Cake
Replace the water with coffee essence or dissolve 2 teaspoons instant coffee powder in 1 tablespoon boiling water.

Lemon or Orange Victoria Sponge Cake
Add the very finely grated rind of 1 lemon or orange.

Victoria sponge cake filled with jam; Madeira cake; Victoria and Madeira cake mixtures

Quick mix cake ingredients

CAKE SIZES	2 (18-cm/7-in) sandwich tins	18 paper cake cases or patty tins	20-cm/8-in sandwich tin / 20-cm/8-in ring mould / 18-cm/7-in deep square tin	*900-ml/1½-pint pudding basin	about 26 paper cake cases or patty tins	2 (20-cm/8-in) sandwich tins	23-cm/9-in sandwich tin
soft (tub) margarine, chilled	100 g/4 oz	100 g/4 oz	100 g/4 oz	100 g/4 oz	175 g/6 oz	175 g/6 oz	175 g/6 oz
caster sugar	100 g/4 oz	100 g/4 oz	100 g/4 oz	100 g/4 oz	175 g/6 oz	175 g/6 oz	175 g/6 oz
eggs (sizes 1, 2)	2	2	2	2	3	3	3
self-raising flour, sifted	100 g/4 oz	100 g/4 oz	100 g/4 oz	100 g/4 oz	175 g/6 oz	175 g/6 oz	175 g/6 oz
baking powder	1 teaspoon	1 teaspoon	1 teaspoon	1 teaspoon	1½ teaspoons	1½ teaspoons	
vanilla essence	4 drops	4 drops	4 drops	4 drops	6 drops	6 drops	6 drops
Approx. cooking time	25–30 minutes	15–20 minutes	35–40 minutes	about 50 minutes	15–20 minutes	30–35 minutes	about 25 minutes

CAKE SIZES	28 × 18 × 4-cm/11 × 7 × 1½-in slab cake / 20-cm/8-in round tin / 20-cm/8-in square tin	*1-litre/2-pint pudding basin	29 × 21 × 4-cm/11½ × 8½ × 1½-in slab cake	23-cm/9-in round tin / 23-cm/9-in square tin	30 × 25 × 5-cm/12 × 10 × 2-in slab cake
soft (tub) margarine, chilled	175 g/6 oz	175 g/6 oz	225 g/8 oz	225 g/8 oz	275 g/10 oz
caster sugar	175 g/6 oz	175 g/6 oz	225 g/8 oz	225 g/8 oz	275 g/10 oz
eggs (sizes 1, 2)	3	3	4	4	5
self-raising flour	175 g/6 oz	175 g/6 oz	225 g/8 oz	225 g/8 oz	275 g/10 oz
baking powder	1½ teaspoons	1½ teaspoons	2 teaspoons	2 teaspoons	2½ teaspoons
vanilla essence	6 drops	6 drops	8 drops	8 drops	10 drops
Approx. cooking time	35–40 minutes	about 1 hour	about 40 minutes	about 1 hour	about 50–60 minutes

*add 25 g/1 oz cornflour sifted with the flour.

QUICK MIX CAKE

Put the margarine, sugar, eggs, flour, baking powder and vanilla essence into a bowl. Mix together with a wooden spoon or hand-held electric mixer, then beat hard for 1–2 minutes until smooth and glossy.

Turn the mixture into a greased and floured tin(s), level the top and bake in a moderate oven (160 c, 325 f, gas 3) for the time suggested in the chart, or until the cake is well-risen, just firm to the touch and beginning to shrink from the sides of the tin.

Turn out on to a wire rack, then invert the cake on to a second wire rack, unless baked in a ring mould or basin. Leave to cool.

Variations

Chocolate Quick Mix Cake
Omit the vanilla essence and add 1 tablespoon sifted cocoa powder for the 2-egg mixture, $1\frac{1}{2}$ tablespoons for the 3-egg mixture, 2 tablespoons for the 4-egg mixture, and $2\frac{1}{2}$ tablespoons for the 5-egg mixture.

Coffee Quick Mix Cake
Omit the vanilla essence and add 2 teaspoons instant coffee powder or 1 tablespoon coffee essence for the 2-egg mixture, 3 teaspoons coffee powder or $1\frac{1}{2}$ tablespoons coffee essence for the 3-egg mixture, 4 teaspoons coffee powder or 2 tablespoons coffee essence for the 4-egg mixture, and 5 teaspoons coffee powder or $2\frac{1}{2}$ tablespoons coffee essence for the 5-egg mixture.

Orange or Lemon Quick Mix Cake
Omit the vanilla essence and add 2 teaspoons finely grated orange or lemon rind for the 2-egg mixture, 3 teaspoons orange or lemon rind for the 3-egg mixture, 4 teaspoons orange or lemon rind for the 4-egg mixture and 5 teaspoons orange or lemon rind for the 5-egg mixture.

WHISKED SPONGE CAKE

Put the eggs and sugar in a heatproof bowl over a saucepan of hot but not boiling water. Whisk until the mixture becomes very thick and pale in colour and the whisk leaves a heavy trail when lifted. Remove the bowl from the saucepan and continue whisking until the cake mixture is cool. Alternatively, the whisking may be done with an electric mixture, without heat.

Sift together the flour and baking powder, then sift again over the whisked mixture. Using a metal spoon, fold in the flour quickly and evenly. Turn into a greased and single-lined tin(s) (see page 5) and shake gently, or spread lightly with a palette knife until level.

Bake in a moderate or moderately hot oven (see chart) for the time suggested, or until the cake springs back when gently pressed with the finger-tips and has begun to shrink a little from the sides of the tin. Turn out on to a wire rack and remove the greaseproof paper. Leave to cool.

If making a Swiss roll, invert the cake on to a sheet of greaseproof paper sprinkled liberally with caster sugar. Quickly peel off the lining paper and trim the edges of the cake with a sharp knife. Fold the top short edge of the cake in about 2.5 cm/1 in, then roll up the cake loosely with the paper inside. (This process must be completed immediately the cake is taken out of the oven for it will not roll up without cracking if it is allowed to cool.) Leave to cool and set for a few minutes, then carefully unroll and remove the paper. Fill with jam, butter cream, or fruit and whipped cream, and roll up again.

Variations

Lemon or Orange Whisked Sponge Cake
Add the grated rind of $\frac{1}{2}$ lemon or orange with the flour.
Chocolate Whisked Sponge Cake
Replace 15 g/$\frac{1}{2}$ oz of the flour with sifted cocoa powder.
Coffee Whisked Sponge Cake
Add 2 teaspoons instant coffee powder with the flour.

LIGHT FRUIT CAKE

This is a moist well-flavoured cake which has grated apple in it to help with the moisture, but it does not keep for longer than about two weeks. It is therefore better to use it only for a simply decorated cake. It can be covered with marzipan as with all fruit cakes and with any of the icings. The currants suggested in the recipe may be replaced with finely chopped, stoned dates or with a mixture of finely chopped, no-need-to-soak dried apricots and stoned, chopped prunes.

Grease and double-line the chosen tin (see page 5). Sift the flour, bicarbonate of soda, spice and ginger into a bowl. In another bowl cream the butter or margarine with the sifted brown sugar until very light, fluffy and pale in colour. Beat in the eggs one at a time, following each with a spoonful of the flour mixture, then fold in the remaining flour.

Mix the raisins, currants, sultanas, peel and fruit rind together and add to the mixture. Peel, core and coarsely grate the apples, add to the mixture

Whisked sponge cake ingredients

CAKE SIZES	2 (18-cm/7-in) sandwich tins	20-cm/8-in sandwich 18-cm/7-in square tin	28 × 18-cm/11 × 7-in Swiss roll tin	18 sponge drops	20-cm/8-in round cake tin	2 × 20-cm/8-in sandwich tins	28 × 18 × 3.5-cm/11 × 7 × 7½-in slab cake	30 × 23-cm/12 × 9-in Swiss roll tin
eggs (sizes 1, 2)	2	2	2	2	3	3	3	3
caster sugar	50 g/2 oz	50 g/2 oz	50 g/2 oz	50 g/2 oz	75 g/3 oz	75 g/3 oz	75 g/3 oz	75 g/3 oz
plain flour	50 g/2 oz	50 g/2 oz	50 g/2 oz	50 g/2 oz	75 g/3 oz	75 g/3 oz	75 g/3 oz	75 g/3 oz
baking powder	$\frac{1}{2}$ teaspoon	$\frac{1}{2}$ teaspoon	$\frac{1}{2}$ teaspoon	$\frac{1}{2}$ teaspoon	$\frac{1}{2}$ teaspoon	$\frac{1}{2}$ teaspoon	$\frac{1}{2}$ teaspoon	$\frac{1}{2}$ teaspoon
Approx. cooking time	*20–25 minutes*	*25–30 minutes*	*10–12 minutes*	*5–10 minutes*	*35–40 minutes*	*20–25 minutes*	*30–35 minutes*	*12–15 minutes*
Oven	*180 C, 350 F, gas 4*	*180 C, 350 F, gas 4*	*190 C, 375 F, gas 5*	*190 C, 375 F, gas 5*	*180 C, 350 F, gas 4*	*180 C, 350 F, gas 4*	*180 C, 350 F, gas 4*	*200 C, 400 F, gas 6*

and stir through to distribute evenly.

Turn the mixture into the prepared tin, level the top and bake in a moderate oven (180 C, 350 F, gas 4) for the time suggested on the chart. The largest size of cake is better if the oven heat is reduced to 160 C, 325 F, gas 3 after 1½ hours to prevent over-browning.

The cake is done when a skewer inserted into the centre comes out clean. Cool in the tin for 5 minutes, then turn out on to a wire rack and leave until cold. When cold wrap in foil or put into an airtight container for 24–48 hours before use.

This fruit cake will keep well in the freezer for up to three months. Do not remove the lining paper from around the cake once it has cooled, but wrap it straight from the tin securely in foil.

Light fruit cake ingredients

CAKE SIZES	18 cm/7 in round 15 cm/6 in square	20 cm/8 in round 18 cm/7 in square	23 cm/9 in round 20 cm/8 in square	25 cm/10 in round 23 cm/9 in square
plain flour	175 g/6 oz	225 g/8 oz	350 g/12 oz	450 g/1 lb
bicarbonate of soda	⅓ teaspoon	½ teaspoon	¾ teaspoon	1 teaspoon
mixed spice	⅓ teaspoon	½ teaspoon	¾ teaspoon	1 teaspoon
ground ginger	good pinch	¼ teaspoon	⅓ teaspoon	½ teaspoon
butter or margarine	100 g/4 oz	175 g/6 oz	250 g/9 oz	350 g/12 oz
light soft brown sugar	100 g/4 oz	175 g/6 oz	250 g/9 oz	350 g/12 oz
eggs	2 (size 3 or 4)	2 (size 1 or 2)	3 (size 1 or 2)	4 (size 1 or 2)
raisins	175 g/6 oz	225 g/8 oz	350 g/12 oz	450 g/1 lb
currants	75 g/3 oz	100 g/4 oz	175 g/6 oz	225 g/8 oz
sultanas	75 g/3 oz	100 g/4 oz	175 g/6 oz	225 g/8 oz
cut mixed peel	40 g/1½ oz	50 g/2 oz	75 g/3 oz	100 g/4 oz
grated orange or lemon rind	1	1	1½–2	2
cooking apple	100 g/4 oz	175 g/6 oz	250 g/9 oz	350 g/12 oz
approx cooking time	1–1¼ hours	1¼–1½ hours	about 1¾ hours	2–2¼ hours

GLACÉ ICING

This is the quickest of icings to make and useful for icing sponge, sandwich and other cakes, as well as small cakes and biscuits. The icing will remain liquid if the bowl is placed in another larger bowl containing hot water.

225 g/8 oz icing sugar
2–4 tablespoons hot water
food colouring and/or flavouring (optional)

Sift the icing sugar into a bowl. Gradually beat in sufficient water to give a smooth icing, thick enough to coat the back of a spoon. Extra water or sugar can be added to achieve the correct consistency.

Add a few drops of food colouring or flavouring, if using. Use at once or place over hot water for a short period.

Alternatively, put all the ingredients into a saucepan and heat gently, stirring, until well mixed and smooth; take care not to overheat or the icing will crystallize.
Makes sufficient to cover the top of a 20-cm/8-in round cake.

Variations

Lemon or Orange Glacé Icing
Use strained fruit juice instead of water. A few drops of food colouring can also be added.
Coffee Glacé Icing
Use a little coffee essence or strong black coffee in place of part of the water.
Chocolate Glacé Icing
Dissolve 2 teaspoons cocoa powder in the water and add to the icing sugar.
Mocha Glacé Icing
Dissolve 1 teaspoon cocoa powder and 2 teaspoons instant coffee powder in the water and add to the icing sugar.

GELATINE ICING

This icing can be used to cover the top and sides of a cake, and for cut out or moulded decorations. It is interchangeable with Fondant Moulding Paste or Icing (see right).

2 teaspoons powdered gelatine
2 tablespoons water
about 575 g/1¼ lb icing sugar
1 egg white
1 teaspoon glycerine
food colouring (optional)

Put the gelatine and water in a heatproof bowl. Place over a saucepan of hot but not boiling water and dissolve the gelatine, stirring occasionally. Remove from the heat and allow to cool.

Sift the icing sugar into another bowl. Add the dissolved gelatine, egg white and glycerine. Mix together with a wooden spoon to form a dough, then knead until smooth, adding extra icing sugar if necessary. Add the food colouring, if using, by kneading into the icing.

The icing can be stored in an airtight container or tightly-sealed polythene bag in a cool place for two to three days before use. If the icing begins to dry out on the surface, dip the container briefly in hot water, leave for 1 hour, then knead well again

Left: Applying gelatine icing or fondant moulding paste;
Right: Glacé icing setting inside non-stick silicone paper

before using. *Makes sufficient to cover a 20-cm/8-in round cake.*

FONDANT MOULDING PASTE OR ICING

Interchangeable with Gelatine Icing (see left), this is simple to use once you get used to its consistency. Use it for modelling all types of animals, figures, flowers, and so on, either by colouring the icing first or by painting with liquid food colourings when completed. It is also suitable for covering all types of cakes except tiered wedding cakes – it will not set firm enough to take the weight of the other tiers.

Liquid glucose or glucose syrup is available from chemist shops.

450 g/1 lb icing sugar
1 egg white
50 g/2 oz liquid glucose
food colouring and/or flavouring (optional)

Sift the icing sugar into a mixing bowl and make a well in the centre. Add the egg white and liquid glucose. Beat with a wooden spoon, gradually pulling in the icing sugar from the sides of the bowl, to give a stiff mixture. Knead the icing thoroughly, mixing in any remaining icing sugar in the bowl to give a smooth and manageable paste. Add colouring and flavouring as desired and extra sifted icing sugar, if necessary.

The icing can be stored in a tightly sealed polythene bag or a plastic container in a cool place for 2–3 days before use.

How to apply fondant moulding paste or gelatine icing to a cake

Attach fondant moulding paste or gelatine icing to a cake covered with Marzipan (see page 16) after brushing the marzipan with egg white, or to a cake without marzipan after brushing with Apricot Glaze (see page 15).

Roll out the icing on a surface dredged with icing sugar, or between two sheets of polythene, to a round or square about 10 cm/4 in larger than the cake top. Support the icing on a rolling pin and place over the top of the cake.

Press the icing on to the sides of the cake, working the icing evenly to the back of the cake. Dip your hands in cornflour and/or icing sugar and rub the surface in a circular movement to give an extra covering. Cut off excess icing.

For square cakes cut out a piece of icing at each corner and mould carefully to give even-shaped corners. Leave to dry.

BUTTER CREAM ICING

This standard recipe can be coloured and flavoured in many ways to complement the type of cake to be iced or filled.

100 g / 4 oz butter or soft (tub) margarine
175–225 g / 6–8 oz icing sugar, sifted
few drops of vanilla essence
1–2 tablespoons milk, top-of-the-milk,
**   evaporated milk or lemon juice**

Cream the butter or margarine until soft. Beat in the sugar a little at a time, adding the vanilla essence and sufficient milk or lemon juice to give a fairly firm but spreading consistency. *Makes sufficient to coat the top and sides of an 18-cm/7-in sandwich cake or fill and cover the top of the cake.*

Variations
Coffee Butter Cream
Omit the vanilla essence and replace 1 tablespoon of the milk with coffee essence or strong black coffee; or beat in 2–3 teaspoons instant coffee powder with the icing sugar.

Chocolate Butter Cream
Add 25–40 g / 1½ oz melted plain chocolate; or dissolve 1–2 tablespoons cocoa powder in a little hot water to give a thin paste, cool and beat into the icing.

Orange or Lemon Butter Cream
Omit the vanilla, replace the milk with orange or lemon juice and add the finely grated rind of one orange or lemon.

Mocha Butter Cream
Dissolve 1–2 teaspoons cocoa powder in 1 tablespoon coffee essence or strong black coffee and add in place of the milk.

Brandy (or other liqueur) Butter Cream
Omit the vanilla essence and replace the milk with brandy, whisky, rum, sherry or any other liqueur. A few drops of an appropriate food colouring can be added.

Almond Butter Cream
Replace the vanilla essence with almond essence and beat in about 2 tablespoons very finely chopped toasted almonds.

Walnut Butter Cream
Beat in 25–50 g/1–2 oz very finely chopped walnuts.

Apricot Butter Cream
Omit the vanilla essence and milk and beat in 3 tablespoons sieved apricot jam, a pinch of grated lemon rind and a squeeze of lemon juice.

Minted Butter Cream
Replace the vanilla essence with peppermint essence. A few drops of green food colouring and three or four crushed minted chocolate matchsticks can be added, too.

Butter cream icing; Rich butter cream; Apricot glaze

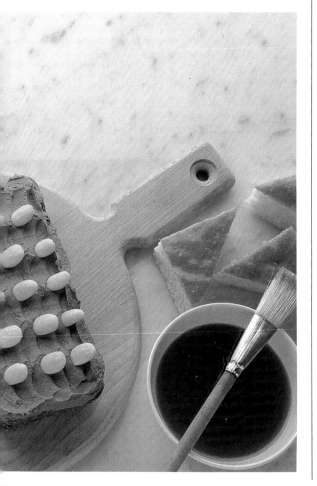

RICH BUTTER CREAM

75 g/3 oz butter
1 egg yolk
225 g/8 oz icing sugar, sifted
1 tablespoon flavouring (orange or lemon juice, coffee essence, for example) or milk

Gently melt the butter in a saucepan. Remove from the heat and beat in the egg yolk.

Gradually beat in the icing sugar, alternating with the flavouring or milk until the mixture is light and fluffy. *Makes sufficient to fill and cover the top of a 20-cm/8-in sandwich cake.*

FUDGE FROSTING

75 g/3 oz butter
3 tablespoons milk
25 g/1 oz soft brown sugar
1 tablespoon black treacle
350 g/12 oz icing sugar, sifted

Put the butter, milk, brown sugar and treacle in a heatproof bowl over a saucepan of hot but not boiling water. Stir occasionally until the butter and sugar have melted, then remove the bowl from the saucepan.

Stir in the icing sugar, then beat with a wooden spoon until the icing is smooth. Pour quickly over a cake for a smooth coating, or leave to cool, then spread over the cake and swirl with a small palette knife. Leave the frosting to set, then decorate as desired.

APRICOT GLAZE

The cool glaze can be stored in an airtight container in the refrigerator for up to one week, but it must be boiled and cooled again before applying it to a cake.

175–225 g/6–8 oz apricot jam
2–3 tablespoons water

Put the jam and water into a saucepan and heat gently until the jam has melted, stirring occasionally. Rub through a sieve and return to a clean pan.

Bring back to the boil and simmer until the required consistency is obtained. Allow to cool.

MARZIPAN OR ALMOND PASTE

This is used for covering all cakes to be coated with royal icing, for decorative tops to cakes, or for moulding animals, flowers, leaves, and other objects for decoration. It can be coloured with liquid, powder or paste food colouring. For a white marzipan use two egg whites instead of an egg or egg yolks.

100 g/4 oz caster sugar
100 g/4 oz icing sugar, sifted
225 g/8 oz ground almonds
1 teaspoon lemon juice
few drops of almond essence
1 egg or 2 egg yolks, beaten

Combine the sugars and ground almonds and make a well in the centre. Add the lemon juice, almond essence and sufficient egg or egg yolks to mix to a firm but manageable dough.

Turn on to a lightly sugared surface and knead until smooth. The marzipan can be wrapped in polythene or foil and stored for two to three days before use.

How to apply marzipan to a cake

The same method is used for both round and square cakes. Make up the required quantity of marzipan for the cake, or use a commercial marzipan.

Place almost half of the marzipan on a working surface dredged with icing sugar, or between two sheets of polythene. Roll out evenly until 2.5 cm/1 in larger than the top of the cake.

Brush the top of the cake with Apricot Glaze (see page 15). Invert the cake on to the marzipan. Using a small palette knife, draw up the edge of the marzipan, attaching it to the sides of the cake and giving an even edge to the top of the cake. Place the cake, marzipan-side up, on a cake board and brush the sides with apricot glaze.

Cut two pieces of string, one the exact height of the cake and the other the complete circumference. Roll out the remaining marzipan to a strip the circumference and height of the cake, or in two shorter strips if easier. Loosely roll the marzipan into a coil. Place one end on the side of the cake and unroll carefully, moulding the marzipan to the side of the cake and making sure the marzipan touches the board.

Using a small palette knife, smooth the join at the ends of the strip and where the strip meets the marzipan on top of the cake. If the marzipan seems unduly moist, rub all over with sifted icing sugar.

Store the cake, uncovered, in a warm dry place for at least 24 hours before applying any icing. For tiered wedding cakes the marzipan should be allowed to dry in the same way for at least a week before icing to prevent the oils from the marzipan seeping into the royal icing during storage after the wedding.

Approximate quantities of marzipan for square and round cakes

SQUARE		15 cm/6 in	18 cm/7 in	20 cm/8 in	23 cm/9 in	25 cm/10 in	28 cm/11 in	30 cm/12 in
ROUND	15 cm/6 in	18 cm/7 in	20 cm/8 in	23 cm/9 in	25 cm/10 in	28 cm/11 in	30 cm/12 in	
Marzipan	350 g/¾ lb	450 g/1 lb	575 g/1¼ lb	800 g/1¾ lb	900 g/2 lb	1 kg/2¼ lb	1.25 kg/2½ lb	1.4 kg/3 lb

How to make a paper icing bag
1. Cut a piece of greaseproof paper to a 25-cm/10-in square. Fold in half to form a triangle. **2.** Fold the triangle in half to make a smaller triangle and press the folds firmly.
3. Open out and fold the bottom half of the triangle up to the folded line, creasing firmly.
4. Continue to fold the bag over and over again, creasing firmly. **5.** Secure the join with clear sticky tape. Cut about 1 cm/½ in off the tip and insert the nozzle.

ROYAL ICING

3 egg whites
about 675 g/1½ lb icing sugar, sifted
2–3 tablespoons strained lemon juice
1–1½ teaspoons glycerine (optional)

Beat the egg whites until frothy, then gradually beat in half the sugar using a wooden spoon. A mixer can be used but it will incorporate a lot of air and the resulting bubbles will be difficult to disperse.

Add the lemon juice, glycerine and half the remaining sugar. Beat well until smooth and very white. Gradually beat in enough of the remaining icing sugar to give a consistency which will just stand in soft peaks.

Put the icing into an airtight container or cover the bowl with a damp cloth and leave for several hours, if possible, to allow most of the air bubbles to come to the surface and burst. The icing is now ready for coating a cake or it can be thickened, for piping stars, flowers, and other decorations, with more sifted icing sugar or thinned down, for flooding, with lightly beaten egg white or strained lemon juice.

Royal icing can be made in any quantity as long as you allow one egg white to each 225 g/8 oz icing sugar. However, it is better to make up not more than a 900 g/2 lb quantity of icing at a time because the icing keeps better if made in small quantities. While using the icing, cover the bowl with a damp cloth to prevent a skin forming. Powdered egg albumen, which is available from specialist cake shops, can be made up according to the instructions on the packet and used in place of fresh egg whites.

Glycerine can be added to help soften the icing and make cutting easier. It should be omitted from the icing for the first couple of coats on the top surface of the bottom tier of a wedding cake and the first coat on the top surface of the middle tier, because a hard surface is needed to take the weight of the other tiers.

The icing can be stored in an airtight container in a cool room for up to two days. It should, however, be stirred very thoroughly before use.

Royal icing – how to flat ice a cake ready for decoration

Approximate quantities of icing sugar used to make royal icing for two thin coats on square and round cakes

SQUARE		15 cm/6 in	18 cm/7 in	20 cm/8 in	23 cm/9 in	25 cm/10 in	28 cm/11 in	30 cm/12 in
ROUND	15 cm/6 in	18 cm/7 in	20 cm/8 in	23 cm/9 in	25 cm/10 in	28 cm/11 in	30 cm/12 in
Icing sugar	450 g/1 lb	575 g/1¼ lb	675 g/1½ lb	900 g/2 lb	1 kg/2¼ lb	1.25 kg/2½ lb	1.4 kg/3 lb	1.6 kg/3½ lb

Some people prefer to ice the top of the cake first and then the sides; others do it the other way round. It doesn't really matter so long as you add several thin coats rather than one thick coat, as this gives the smoothest surface. It is wise to apply the icing in sections rather than all in one go, allowing each application time to dry before continuing.

An ordinary royal iced cake requires two coats on the top and sides. Sometimes an extra coat on the top is necessary if it is not as smooth as you would like. A wedding cake, however requires three coats all over, with an extra coat on the top for the lower tiers.

To ice the top of the cake

Place the cake on a cake board, attaching it with a dab of icing. Put a quantity of icing in the centre of the cake and smooth out with a palette knife, using a paddling movement. Remove surplus icing from the edges.

Draw an icing ruler or long palette knife across the cake towards you carefully and evenly, keeping the rule or knife at an angle of about 30°. Take care not to press too heavily or unevenly. Remove surplus icing by running the palette knife around the top edge of the cake, holding it at right angles to the cake.

If not sufficiently smooth, cover with a little more icing and draw the ruler or knife across the cake again until smooth. Leave to dry.

To ice the sides of the cake

Place the cake on an icing turntable if possible, or use an upturned plate.

For a round cake, spread a thin but covering layer of icing all round the sides of the cake. Again use a paddling action to push out as much air as possible, keeping the icing fairly smooth.

Hold an icing comb or scraper or a palette knife at an angle of about 45° to the cake. Starting at the back of the cake, with your free hand slowly rotate the cake, at the same time moving the comb slowly and evenly round the sides of the cake. Remove the comb at an angle and fairly quickly so the join is hardly noticeable.

Lift any excess icing from the top of the cake using a palette knife, again rotating the cake. If not sufficiently smooth, wipe the comb and repeat. Leave to dry.

For a square cake the best way of achieving good even corners is to ice two opposite sides first, and then when dry to ice the other two. Spread some icing on one side, then draw the comb or palette knife towards you, keeping the cake still to give an even side. Cut off the icing down the corner in a straight line and also off the top and base of the cake.

Repeat with the opposite side and leave to dry. Repeat the process with the two remaining sides, keeping the corners neat and tidy, and leave to dry.

Second and third coats

Repeat the same method for the top and sides when applying each subsequent coat, but make sure each layer is dry before adding the next or you may disturb the previous coats. This will take about three to four hours, but can vary according to the room atmosphere. Leave the cake to dry, uncovered, for 24 hours before adding the decoration.

To ice the cake board

Complete the base-icing of the cake and leave to dry. Stand the cake on an icing turntable and coat the board with a thin layer of icing (it may spread more easily if thinned slightly with a little egg white or lemon juice). Either run a palette knife round the edge while revolving the cake or hold an icing comb at an angle to the icing while rotating. Remove surplus icing from the edge of the board with a palette knife. With a square cake use the same method but ice two opposite sides, leave them to dry then complete the other two sides.

Children's Novelty Cakes

OVER THE RAINBOW

2-egg quantity Quick Mix Cake mixture (pages 8–9)
1 quantity Fondant Moulding Paste (page 13)
red, yellow, blue, green and violet food colourings
2 tablespoons Apricot Glaze (page 15)
cornflour for dusting
1 (30-cm/12-in) thin silver cake board
25 g/1 oz desiccated coconut (optional)
flowers made from Fondant Moulding Paste to decorate (optional)

Base-line and grease a 20-cm/8-in sandwich tin (see page 5), spoon in the cake mixture and bake in

a moderate oven (160 c, 325 f, gas 3) for 35–40 minutes until well risen and firm to the touch. Turn out on to a wire rack, remove paper, and leave to cool.

Make the fondant moulding paste and divide it into eight pieces. Using the food colourings to blend the colours, colour one piece red, one orange (with yellow and red), one yellow, one green, one blue, one indigo (with blue and a little violet) and one piece violet, leaving one piece white. Wrap each piece separately in cling film until required.

Using a 7.5-cm/3-in plain cutter, cut a round out of the centre of the cake and remove. Cut the cake and the small round in half. (See small picture, left.) Reserve the two small semi-circles

of cake. Sandwich the rainbow shapes together with apricot glaze. Brush the underside of the rainbow with glaze. Roll out the white moulding paste and cover the arch underneath the rainbow. Trim to fit. Place the rainbow the right way up and brush with apricot glaze.

Dust the work surface with plenty of cornflour and roll out the red moulding paste, then cut a 1-cm/$\frac{1}{2}$-in-wide strip. Place over the centre join of the cake (see small picture, left) and trim to fit. Knead the trimmings together. Roll out the orange moulding paste, cut out two 1-cm/$\frac{1}{2}$-in-wide strips and place one on either side of the red strip. Trim to fit, kneading the trimmings. Continue by cutting out two yellow, two green, two blue, two indigo and two violet strips. Carefully apply them to each side of the cake. Trim to fit and knead all the trimmings together, keeping the colours separate. Repeat, if wished, to cover the remaining semi-circles to make two mini rainbows.

If liked, serve the rainbow cakes set out on a cake board. Brush the cake board with apricot glaze. Colour the coconut green with a few drops of food colouring and sprinkle all over the board to cover evenly.

Any trimmings of the coloured fondant moulding paste may also be used, if liked, to make moulded flowers to decorate the desiccated coconut 'grass' on the cake board. Press out small petal shapes from the trimmings (see page 42), join three petals together and trim off the stalks.

TREASURE ISLAND

3-egg quantity Quick Mix Cake mixture (pages 8–9)
1 quantity Fudge Frosting (page 15)
1 (25-cm/10-in) thin round silver cake board
2 tablespoons demerara sugar
blue and green decorating gels
2 jelly feet
1 jelly crocodile
5 curl biscuits
1 tablespoon coconut
green food colouring
50 g/2 oz Marzipan (page 16)
5 pieces Swiss milk chocolate with soft filling
milk chocolate coins
jelly sweets
gold and silver almonds
2.5-cm/1-in square rice paper
black food colouring pen

Line and grease a 28 × 18 × 3.5-cm/11 × 7 × 1½-in oblong tin (see page 5), spoon in the cake mixture and bake in a moderate oven (160 c, 325 f, gas 3) for 40–45 minutes until well risen and firm to the touch. Turn out on to a wire rack, remove the paper, and leave to cool.

Cut pieces out of the cake to give it an island shape and place on to the cake board. Reserve the pieces. Make the fudge frosting. Spread about two-thirds of the frosting evenly all over the top and sides of the cake. Spread the remaining cake pieces with frosting and arrange around and on top of the cake to resemble rocks.

Sprinkle the demerara sugar around the cake board and on the rocks at the base of the cake. Squeeze the blue gel on the remaining cake board to make the sea. Squeeze some green gel over the rocks by the sea edge for seaweed. Place the jelly feet as footprints in the sand and the crocodile in the sea. Press the curl biscuits into the top of the cake by the rocks to make tree trunks. Colour the coconut green with a few drops of food colouring, and then spoon the coconut round the trees. Colour the marzipan green with food colouring, then mould 15–18 palm leaves and snip the sides with a pair of scissors. Gently push two or three leaves into the top of each tree trunk to attach.

Using a little frosting, stick four pieces of chocolate together to make a chest and press into the centre of the cake. Place the remaining piece of chocolate resting at the side for a lid. Fill the chest with the chocolate coins, jelly sweets and almonds and press some extras into the cake. Make a map out of the rice paper, marking it with the food colouring pen.

BEACH TIME

3-egg quantity Quick Mix Cake mixture (pages 8–9)
1 quantity Butter Cream (page 14)
blue food colouring
1 (30-cm/12-in) square cake board
225 g/8 oz assorted nuts coated in white milk chocolate, or raisins coated in yogurt
2 tablespoons demerara sugar
20 orange sticks
3 cocktail umbrellas
1 strip strawberry-flavoured liquorice
2 large and 3 small jelly babies
2 pairs of jelly trainers
2 jelly mermaids

Line and grease a 28 × 18 × 3.5-cm/11 × 7 × 1½-in oblong tin, spoon in the cake mixture and bake in a moderate oven (160 c, 325 f, gas 3) for 40–45

minutes until well risen and firm to the touch. Turn out on to a wire rack, remove paper, and leave to cool.

Make the butter cream and colour one-third pale blue. Cut the cake according to the diagram, right. Place the deep part of the cake at the back of the cake board and invert the second piece at the front. Spread two-thirds of the cake with plain butter cream evenly over the sides, back and top. Press the nuts or raisins into the top third of the cake to represent the pebbled part of the beach. Sprinkle the centre with demerara sugar as sand, and spread the blue butter cream on the remaining cake surface in peaks as the sea.

For breakwaters, press 12 orange sticks, spaced apart, down two opposite sides of the cake and using a little plain butter cream secure the remaining sticks in between. Place the cocktail umbrellas, liquorice beach mats, jelly babies, trainers and mermaids to create a lively beach scene.

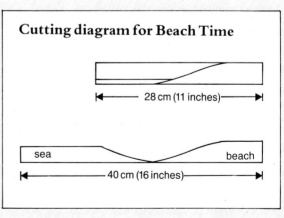

Cutting diagram for Beach Time

|←— 28 cm (11 inches) —→|

sea — beach

|←——— 40 cm (16 inches) ———→|

23

LUNCH BOX AND FLASK

2-egg quantity Quick Mix Cake mixture (pages 8–9)
2-egg quantity Whisked Sponge Cake (page 10)
1 quantity Butter Cream (page 14)
yellow, red and green food colourings
175 g/6 oz Marzipan (page 16)
4 tablespoons Apricot Glaze (page 15)
1 25-cm/10-in square thin silver cake board
2 mini milk chocolate fudge bars

Line and grease a $28 \times 18 \times 3.5$-cm/$11 \times 7 \times 1\frac{1}{2}$-in oblong tin, spoon in the Quick Mix cake mixture and bake in a moderate oven (160 c, 325 F, gas 3) for 30–35 minutes until well risen and firm to the touch. Turn out on to a wire rack, remove the paper, and leave to cool.

Line and grease a 28×18-cm/11×7-in Swiss roll tin, spoon in the Whisked Sponge Cake and bake on a shelf just above the oblong cake for 10–15 minutes. Follow the instructions for making a Swiss roll on page 10.

Make the butter cream and colour it bright yellow with the yellow food colouring. Knead some red food colouring into two-thirds of the marzipan until it is bright red. Colour the remaining marzipan a bright apple green.

Cut the oblong cake in half and sandwich with apricot glaze (see the diagram below) and cut a 5-cm/2-in slice off the Swiss roll and discard (or eat).

Brush both cakes with apricot glaze and place on the cake board. Carefully spread the yellow butter cream smoothly and evenly over the oblong cake, using a palette knife dipped in hot water. Coat the Swiss roll evenly the same way and stand it on end next to the oblong cake. Leave in a cool place to set.

Roll out a 3.5×23-cm/$1\frac{1}{2} \times 9$-in strip of red marzipan. Carefully place around the top end of the Swiss roll and join carefully. Cut out a 6-cm/$2\frac{1}{2}$-in round of marzipan and place in position on top of the Swiss roll. Mould a small marzipan handle and leave to set. Cut one of the fudge bars in half and cover the complete bar and the two pieces in red marzipan. Position as a handle on the lunch box using the two small pieces as handle supports.

Roll out the remaining red marzipan thinly and cut out 5-mm/$\frac{1}{4}$-in strips. Use to trim the edges and base of the lunch box. Place a red strip of marzipan across the top and down the side of the lunch box and mark the opening line with a knife. Cut out the lock and the letters for the name of the child with an alphabet cutter. Using any patterned cutter, cut out some shapes and press in position on the lunch box and flask. Attach the handle to the cup on the flask with glaze.

Mould an apple shape from the green marzipan, and decorate with a leaf made from a diamond-shaped piece of marzipan, its edges pressed into a leaf form, and with veins marked on.

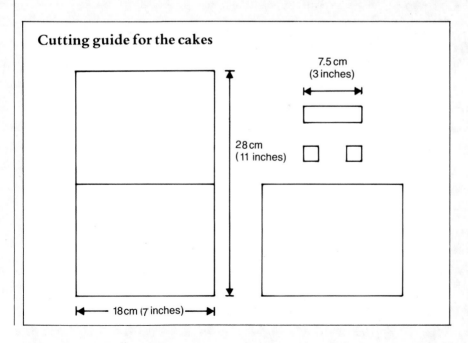

Cutting guide for the cakes

7.5 cm (3 inches)

28 cm (11 inches)

18 cm (7 inches)

SUGAR PLUM FAIRY CASTLE

6-egg quantity Whisked Sponge Cake mixture (page 10)
6 tablespoons Apricot Glaze (page 15)
1½ quantity Fondant Moulding Paste (page 13)
pink food colouring
50 g/2 oz quantity Quick Mix Cake mixture (pages 8–9)
400 g/14 oz sugar
2 teaspoons cold water
cornflour for sprinkling
1 (30-cm/12-in) fluted round silver cake board
pink food colouring pen
225 g/8 oz sugared almonds

Line and grease a 33 × 23-cm/13 × 9-in Swiss roll tin and a 28 × 18-cm/11 × 7-in Swiss roll tin. Place two-thirds of the whisked sponge mixture in the larger tin and one-third in the smaller tin. Bake in a moderate oven (180 c, 350 f, gas 4) for 15–20 minutes until well risen and firm to the touch.

Use some of the apricot glaze as filling and roll up following the instructions for making a Swiss roll (see page 10) but roll the smaller Swiss roll lengthways to make a long thin roll. Make the fondant moulding paste and tint it very pale pink with a few drops of food colouring, then wrap it in cling film.

Line and grease a 20-cm/8-in sandwich tin and add the quick mix cake mixture. Bake in a moderate oven (180 c, 350 f, gas 4) for 15–20 minutes until well risen and firm to the touch. Turn out on to a wire rack to cool.

Place the sugar in a bowl, add a drop of pink food colouring to tint it the same colour as the fondant moulding paste. Reserve one-third of the sugar and add the water to the remainder. Mix together well so that the sugar becomes damp. Make three cone shapes out of paper (see small picture, right). Fill the large cone with the dampened sugar and press firmly down. Place a piece of card over the top and invert the sugar cone, then remove the paper shape. Repeat to make one medium and two small cones and leave in a warm place to dry hard.

Trim the ends of each Swiss roll so that they are level. Cut one-third off each roll to make four towers all of different heights (see diagram, right). Unwrap the moulding paste and cut into five pieces. Roll out one piece thinly on a surface well sprinkled with cornflour, the width of the largest roll and long enough to roll completely around it. Brush the roll with some of the remaining apricot

glaze, place it on the moulding paste, trim the moulding paste to fit, then roll up, carefully sealing the join by rubbing over it with cornfloured fingers. Repeat to cover the remaining rolls. Knead and re-roll the trimmings. Place the reserved sugar on a piece of greaseproof paper and roll each iced roll in it to coat evenly. Leave to dry.

Place the round cake on the cake board and, using plain cutters the same size as the base of each roll, cut out and remove four rounds. Brush the cake with some more of the apricot glaze and roll

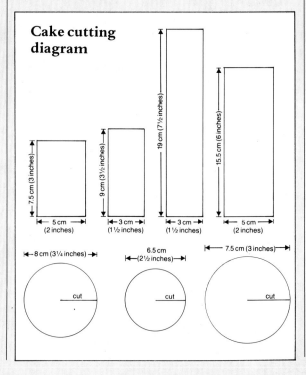

Cake cutting diagram

out the remaining moulding paste to a circle large enough to cover the round cake. Place the moulding paste over the cake, and gently press it into the holes.

Smooth over and trim off the excess at the base. Sprinkle the moulding paste and cake board with the remaining pink-tinted sugar. Place each pink tower in position in the cut-out holes and carefully place the sugar cones on top of each. Make the windows and doors for the towers with the fondant moulding paste trimmings (as in the main picture) and use the pink pen to mark the lattice work and door panels. Place these in position and secure with the remaining apricot glaze. Arrange the sugared almonds like a path and steps into the castle.

BALLET SHOES

**3-egg quantity Whisked Sponge Cake mixture
    (page 10)**
3 tablespoons Apricot Glaze (page 15)
1 quantity Fondant Moulding Paste (page 13)
pink and yellow food colourings
4 ice cream wafers
1 metre/1 yard 1-cm/½-in-wide peach ribbon
1 (20-cm/8-in) round thin silver cake board

Line and grease a 33 × 23-cm/13 × 9-in Swiss roll
tin, spoon in the cake mixture and bake in a
moderate oven (180 c, 350 f, gas 4) for 10–15
minutes until well risen and firm to the touch.

Turn out the cake on to a piece of sugared
greaseproof paper. Remove the lining paper and
trim off the edges of the cake. Quickly spread
with some of the apricot glaze and roll up from
the long edge. Cool on a wire rack. Make the
fondant moulding paste and add a few drops of
pink and yellow food colourings to make it
peach-coloured.

Cut the wafers out to form the soles of the
shoes. Cut the Swiss roll in half and press one end
of each into a point. Cut out a shallow oval shape
from the centre of each roll, then brush both all
over with most of the remaining glaze.

Cut the icing in half and roll out one half large
enough to cover one roll. Use this icing to cover
one of the rolls completely, join on the underside,
and neaten the edges. Shape the heel and toe of the
shoe until smooth. Brush the wafer sole with glaze
and press into position on the ballet shoe, trimming to fit if necessary. Using well-cornfloured
hands, press the icing into the oval depression in
the centre of the shoe and form a sharp edge all
around the top with the fingers. Make an icing
bow from the peach icing trimmings. Make into a
pencil-thin roll, fold into two loops, trim and
place in position on the toe with glaze. Repeat the
process for the other shoe.

Cut the ribbon into four pieces; press in
position at the back of each shoe and secure with
icing. Arrange the ballet shoes on the cake board.

Petal candle holders, made from icing trimmings, may be made for this cake, if liked. Take a
small ball of icing and press into a petal shape, curl
the edge of the petal inwards to form a centre.
Press out another petal shape and wrap around the
centre petal; repeat with a third petal, then cut off
the stem. Press the candle into the centre. Repeat
to make as many candle holders as required, then
place beside the ballet shoes.

How to use the fondant moulding paste

As the Swiss roll is very fragile when it is first made, leave it to settle for a day before making the ballet shoes.

When rolling out the fondant moulding paste, take care not to roll it out too thinly, otherwise the cake may show through and the moulding paste will be difficult to handle when it is being moulded into the shape of the ballet shoes.

DENNIS DINOSAUR

2-egg quantity Quick Mix Cake mixture (pages 8–9)
peppermint essence
green food colouring
1 quantity Fondant Moulding Paste (page 13)
2 tablespoons Apricot Glaze (page 15)
2 mini chocolate Swiss rolls
3 sweet cigarettes
red dragees
2 strips strawberry flavour liquorice

Make the cake mixture, adding a few drops of peppermint essence and green food colouring. Base-line and grease a 20-cm/8-in round sandwich tin, spoon in the cake mixture and bake in a moderate oven (160 c, 325 f, gas 3) for 40–45 minutes until well risen and firm to the touch. Turn out on to a wire rack, remove the paper, and leave to cool.

Make the fondant moulding paste and colour it green with a few drops of food colouring. Using a 7.5-cm/3-in plain cutter, cut a round out from the centre of the cake and reserve. Cut the cake into two half circles and sandwich together with some of the apricot glaze, following the diagram opposite. Roll out two-thirds of the fondant moulding paste and cover the cake completely, carefully sealing the joins underneath the arched body shape.

Cut the mini Swiss rolls in half to make four legs and cut the reserved round piece of cake in half. Use one half for a head, then cut the other semi-circle in half for the tail pieces, as in the diagram below. Roll out the remaining moulding paste and carefully cover the legs, head and tail pieces. Leave all the pieces to set for at least 1 hour in a warm place or preferably overnight.

Arrange the legs on a long board or tray and brush the tops with some of the remaining apricot glaze. Place the body in position. Press two sweet cigarettes a little way into the head end and one into the tail end, brush the head and one tail piece with glaze at one end and press into position on the body (see small picture, left). Attach the remaining tail piece with glaze. Using the red dragees, press into the head for eyes and mouth. Cut the liquorice strips in half, then into diamond shapes. Press these into the icing all over the head, back and tail to represent spines. Cut the remaining pieces of liquorice into tiny toe nails and stick them around the feet with the remaining apricot glaze.

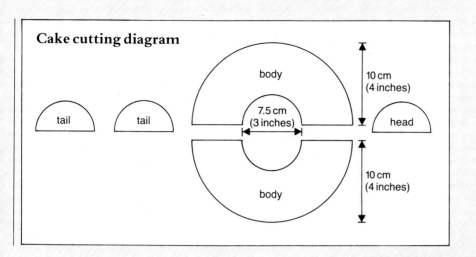

Cake cutting diagram

body

7.5 cm
(3 inches)

body

10 cm
(4 inches)

10 cm
(4 inches)

tail

tail

head

SAMMY SNAKE

3-egg quantity Whisked Sponge Cake mixture (page 10)
3 tablespoons Apricot Glaze (page 15)
1 quantity Fondant Moulding Paste (page 13)
blue, green and orange food colourings
2 green jelly diamonds, cut in half
2 orange jelly diamonds

Line and grease a 33 × 23-cm/13 × 9-in Swiss roll tin, spoon in the cake mixture and bake in a moderate oven (180 c, 350 F, gas 4) for 10–15 minutes until well risen and firm to the touch. Turn out the cake on to a piece of sugared greaseproof paper. Remove lining paper and trim off the edges. Quickly brush with some of the apricot glaze and roll up one long edge to the centre. Place a rolling pin behind as a support. Roll the opposite edge into the centre (see small picture, top right).

Leave to set for a couple of minutes, then cut the cake in half down the centre to make 2 long thin rolls. Place the rolls on a wire rack and bend each roll into an 'S' shape (see small picture, bottom right). Make the fondant moulding paste and colour three-quarters of it turquoise blue using a few drops of blue and green food colourings. Colour the remaining moulding paste orange. Place the two rolls on a long tray or board and brush the two ends with glaze to join them together. Brush the roll all over with glaze.

Roll out the turquoise blue moulding paste into a long thin strip, 2.5 cm/1 in longer than the snake. Cover the snake with the moulding paste, shaping it carefully to form the tail at one end and the head at the other and pressing gently to fit. Slit the icing at the head end to form the mouth. Use a little of the orange icing to line the mouth and to make a forked tongue; place in the mouth. Roll out the remaining orange moulding paste and cut into thin strips. Cut the strips into short lengths and arrange at intervals across the body as stripes. Cut two dots for the eyes and place in position.

Use the green jelly diamonds for teeth. Place the orange jelly diamonds on the head.

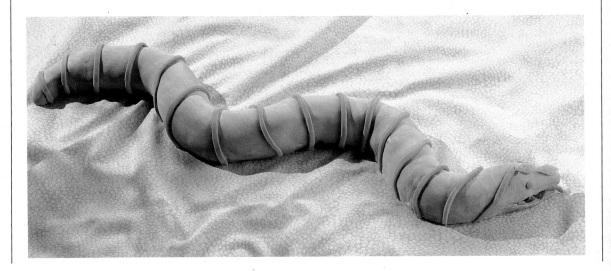

TOBY TRANSFORMER

3-egg quantity Quick Mix Cake mixture (pages 8–9)
1 quantity Fondant Moulding Paste (page 13)
red and black food colourings
2 tablespoons Apricot glaze (page 15)
1 (30-cm/12-in) thin square silver cake board

Line and grease a 28 × 18 × 3.5-cm/11 × 7 × 1½-in oblong tin, spoon in the cake mixture and bake in a moderate oven (160 c, 325 f, gas 3) for 50–55 minutes until well risen and firm to the touch. Turn out on to a wire rack, remove paper, and leave to cool.

Cut out the cake according to the diagram below and assemble the pieces in the correct order. Make the fondant moulding paste and colour one-third red and two-thirds grey with a few drops of red and black food colourings. Roll out the red paste thinly, brush the booster jets and body with apricot glaze, then cover each piece

with red moulding paste and trim to fit. Using some grey moulding paste, roll and cut out the trims for the body and place in position.

Roll out the remaining grey paste and cover all the remaining parts of the transformer, glazing them first with apricot glaze. Trim the head and arms with a strip of red paste. Arrange the pieces in order on the cake board.

Cake cutting diagram

5 cm (2 inches)

3 cm (1¼ inches)

6.5 cm (2½ inches)

7.5 cm (3 inches)

6.5 cm (2½ inches)

6.5 cm (2½ inches)

10 cm (4 inches)

2.5 cm (1 inch)

2.5 cm (1 inch)

HUMPTY DUMPTY

3-egg quantity Chocolate Quick Mix Cake mixture (pages 8–9)
1 quantity Butter Cream (page 14)
1 tablespoon cocoa powder
2 teaspoons boiling water
pink, blue, green and yellow food colourings
50 g/2 oz desiccated coconut
4 tablespoons Apricot Glaze (page 15)
2 (20-cm/8-in) thick silver cake boards
25 g/1 oz liquorice comfits
1 tablespoon chocolate flavour toasted rice
50 g/2 oz Marzipan (page 16)
black food colouring pen (optional)
1 sheet rice paper (optional)

Base-line and grease a 1.15-litre/2-pint pudding basin, an 18-cm/7-in round sandwich tin and a 450-g/1-lb loaf tin. Place two tablespoonsful of the cake mixture in the basin, and divide the remainder between the two tins. Bake in a moderate oven (160 C, 325 F, gas 3) for about 30 minutes for the basin and round tin, and 40–45 minutes for the loaf tin, until well risen and firm to the touch. Turn out on to a wire rack, remove the paper, and leave to cool.

Make the butter cream and divide into three portions. Blend the cocoa and water together and cool, then beat it into one-third of the butter cream. Colour another third of the butter cream pink and the remaining third blue with the appropriate food colourings. Reserve one tablespoon of coconut, divide the remainder into three and colour one-third blue, one-third green and one-third yellow by adding a few drops of each food colouring to a portion of coconut and mixing until well blended.

Brush the cake board with apricot glaze and sprinkle over the coloured coconut to make a background picture (see pictures, left). Spread the top and sides of the oblong cake with the chocolate butter cream, place on the cake board 1 cm/½ in from the bottom and mark the butter cream to resemble a brick wall.

Sandwich the round and pudding basin cakes together with apricot glaze and spread half with pink and half with blue butter cream. Place on the board against the top of the wall. Arrange the sweets across the middle of the cake to form a 'belt', and also place the eyes, nose and mouth in position. Press the toasted rice in position for hair.

Colour half the marzipan pink and half blue with food colourings and shape the pink into arms and the blue into legs. Place in position on the cake.

The second cake board may be used, if liked, to add the Humpty Dumpty nursery rhyme to the cake. Brush a 7.5-cm/3-in border of apricot glaze on the board and sprinkle with tinted desiccated coconut. Use the food colouring pen to write the rhyme on the rice paper and secure it to the cake board, inside the coconut border, with a little glaze.

CIRCUS RING

2-egg quantity Quick Mix Cake mixture (pages 8–9)

½ quantity Fondant Moulding Paste (page 13)

red, yellow, green, blue, black and purple food colourings

1 (25-cm/10-in) thin round silver cake board

1 tablespoon Apricot Glaze (page 15)

3 tablespoons light soft brown sugar

2 candy sticks

1 piece strawberry flavour liquorice

8 edible circus wafers

1 clown, 2 elephants, 2 seals with balls, made from moulding paste (see method) or use bought figures

Base-line and grease a 20-cm/8-in sandwich tin, and spoon in the cake mixture. Bake in a moderate oven (160 c, 325 f, gas 3) for 35–40 minutes until well risen and firm to the touch. Turn out on to a wire rack, remove the paper and leave to cool.

Make the fondant moulding paste. Reserve one-third and cut the remaining two-thirds into six pieces. Colour the pieces red, yellow, green and blue with the food colourings. Wrap each piece in cling film until used.

Place the cake on the board and brush it all over with apricot glaze. Mark the cake on the outside edge into eight equal sections. Roll out and trim two pieces of red moulding paste to fit two side sections of the cake. Press one piece in position, then the remaining piece on the opposite side. Repeat with the blue, yellow and green moulding paste, so that the outside of the cake is covered in

alternating coloured sections. Knead the trimmings together, keeping the colours separate, then mould each colour into two square-edge lengths to fit each section. To do this, make a roll from each colour then flatten to make a four-sided shape. Place the edging pieces around the top edge of the cake, matching the side colours.

Sprinkle the top of the cake with sugar. Press the candy sticks into the cake, one at each side. Cut a thin strip of red liquorice and tie it around the candy sticks to make a tight rope. Stick the circus wafers on to the outside of the cake, one on each of the coloured sections.

Mould the clown from multi-coloured moulding paste. To do this, take a piece of white paste the size of a walnut and press small balls of red, yellow, green and blue paste on to it. Roll gently to blend all the colours together and mould into a clown (see small picture, left). Colour half the remaining white moulding paste greyish purple, using black and purple food colourings. Mould two elephants, using coloured icing trimmings to make their hats. Colour the reserved moulding paste black and use to make two seals and balls. Leave to set, then place the animals in the circus ring.

most of the butter cream icing
the centre of the cake
biscuit pie...
Secu...
the l...
sides,...
before...

Knea...
the ma...
mainder...

BUNNY BIG EARS

2-egg quantity Quick Mix Cake mixture (pages 8–9)
50 g/2 oz chocolate dots
175 g/6 oz Fondant Moulding Paste (page 13)
blue, orange and green food colourings
1 quantity Butter Cream (page 14)
25 g/1 oz desiccated coconut
2 tablespoons Apricot Glaze (page 15)
1 20-cm/8-in round thin silver cake board
blue food colouring pen
1 sheet of rice paper

Base-line and grease a 20-cm/8-in round cake tin. Make the quick mix cake mixture and stir in the chocolate dots. Place in the prepared tin and bake in a moderate oven (160 C, 325 F, gas 3) for 40–45 minutes until well risen and firm to the touch. Turn out on to a wire rack, remove the paper, and leave to cool.

Make the fondant moulding paste. Colour three-quarters pale blue with a few drops of blue food colouring and use to shape two back legs and two front feet, two eyes and a nose. Leave to set. Use half the remaining moulding paste to make a round tail. Colour most of the remainder orange; shape this into a carrot. Colour a little icing with green food colouring and use to make the carrot leaves. Press into position.

Make the butter cream and tint pale blue. Colour two-thirds of the coconut pale blue and one-third green with the food colourings. Cut the cake in half (see diagram below) and sandwich together with apricot glaze. Place the cake on the board.

Brush the whole cake with apricot glaze and press the legs and feet in position. Using a palette knife, cover the whole of the cake with blue butter cream to coat evenly. Cover the cake with blue coconut, brushing the excess off the board. Brush the remaining board with glaze and sprinkle with green coconut.

Press the tail, eyes and nose on to the face and highlight the eyes and nose with the blue pen. Place the carrot in position. Cut two large ears (shaped as in diagram below) and six thin whiskers from the rice paper and place in position.

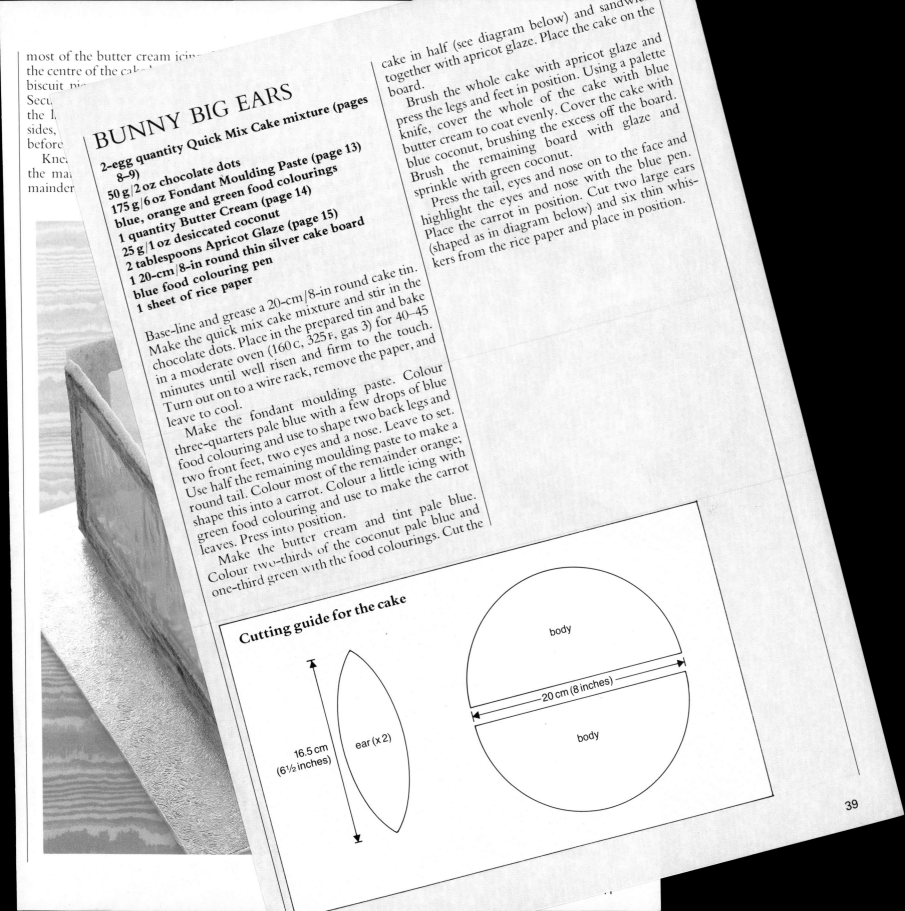

Cutting guide for the cake

16.5 cm (6½ inches)

ear (x 2)

body

20 cm (8 inches)

body

Cakes for Special Occasions

WINDOW BOX

3-egg quantity Quick Mix Cake mixture (pages 8–9)
½ quantity Fondant Moulding Paste (page 13)
green, pink, yellow and orange food colourings
cornflour
½ quantity Chocolate Butter Cream (page 14)
1 (20-cm/8-in) square silver cake board
2 (150-g/5-oz) packets chocolate finger biscuits

Line and grease a 1-kg/2-lb loaf tin and add the cake mixture. Bake in a moderate oven (160 c,

Cutting diagrams for

side (x

(½ inch)
1 cm

7 cm
(2¾ inches)

1 cm
(½ inch)

20 cm (8 inch

325ꜰ, gas 3) for 50–55 minutes until well risen and firm to the touch. Turn out, remove paper and cool on a wire rack.

Make the fondant moulding paste, divide into four equal portions, then colour each piece with a few drops of food colouring, so that the portions are tinted green, pink, yellow and orange. Roll out the green moulding paste. Cut out 20 leaves, marking the veins with a knife, bend slightly, then leave to dry on a plate dusted with cornflour. Re-roll the trimmings.

To make 22 pink flowers (see small picture, bottom right) take small balls of the pink mould-ing paste, then press out three round petal shapes for each flower between thumb and forefinger. Fold the petals inwards, then gently press the three petals together to complete the flower and leave to set. Using the yellow moulding paste, press out 20 larger yellow petals and fold inwards, leaving a stem attached (see small picture, below). Next take the orange moulding paste and press out into twelve large round shapes with a stem and press a green piece, taken from the leaf trimmings, into each centre (see picture, below). Leave all the flowers and leaves to set hard.

Make the chocolate butter cream and spread

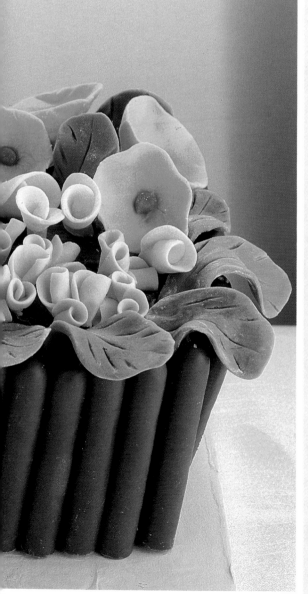

evenly over the sides and top of the cake. Place on the cake board. Trim and fit the chocolate finger biscuits all around the sides of the cake, leaving the fingers at the back the full length as these will be needed to support the large orange flowers at the back of the box. Arrange the leaves around the edges of the window box. Place the pink flowers at the front, then arrange the yellow flowers, and finally arrange the large orange flowers at the back, supported by the chocolate fingers.

EXECUTIVE CASE

3-egg quantity Coffee Quick Mix Cake mixture (pages 8–9)
1 quantity Fondant Moulding Paste (page 13)
violet, blue, red and gold food colourings
2 tablespoons Apricot Glaze (page 15)
1 (20-cm/8-in) square thin silver cake board
1 oblong wafer biscuit
black food colouring pen
1 blackcurrant candy stick
2 sheets of rice paper

Line and grease a 26 × 19 × 5-cm/10½ × 7½ × 2-in oblong tin, spoon in the cake mixture and bake in a moderate oven (160 c, 325 f, gas 3) for 50–55 minutes until well risen and firm to the touch.

Turn out on to a wire rack, remove the paper, and leave to cool.

Make the moulding paste. Reserve a small piece and colour the remainder a brown-burgundy colour by adding violet, blue and red food colourings. Cut the cake in half across the width, sandwich together with apricot glaze and trim the top square. Brush with apricot glaze and place on the cake board. Roll out one-third of the burgundy coloured moulding paste to a 13-cm/5-in square. Cut the square in half and place each piece down the side of the case. Trim to fit. Roll out the remaining piece of burgundy paste large enough to cover the case. Carefully fit the paste over the case and trim to fit, neatly joining the edges together. Mark a line across the top and down the side for the opening seam.

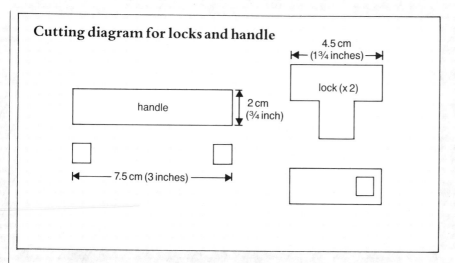

4.5 cm
(1¾ inches)

lock (x 2)

handle

2 cm
(¾ inch)

7.5 cm (3 inches)

Cover the biscuit with trimmings of burgundy moulding paste for the handle (see diagram, above) and roll, cut and trim a 3.5-cm/1½-in square for the label. Roll out the white moulding paste and cut out two locks, two handle supports (see diagram, above) and the initials and paint with gold food colouring. Leave to set. Cut out the name tag from the white paste. Reserve the trimmings. Secure the locks in place with a little glaze, and the handle and supports. With a food colouring pen, write the name and address of the recipient on the name tag, then stick together with the label. Fix the label in position under the handle.

Re-roll the burgundy moulding paste trimmings into a 15-cm/6-in round. Place the candy stick in the centre, then pleat the remaining paste around like an umbrella (see pictures, left). With the white paste trimmings, make a handle and top for the umbrella and trim with gold food colouring. Leave to set, then place on the cake board.

Using the rice paper and colouring pen, make a newspaper and write the day and date of the celebration, favourite newspaper title and a few lines written in columns. Place by the case.

CHESS BOARD

**1 (20-cm/8-in) square Light Fruit Cake
  (pages 10–11)
1 (25-cm/10-in) square silver cake board
4 tablespoons Apricot Glaze (page 15)
675 g/1½ lb Marzipan (page 16)
1½ quantities Fondant Moulding Paste (page 13)
brown and back food colourings**

Place the cake on the board and trim the top if necessary to make it level. Brush the top and sides with apricot glaze, then cover with the marzipan.

Trim, reserving the trimmings.

Make the fondant moulding paste. Divide it in half and colour one half brown with a few drops of brown food colouring. Leave the other half cream. Colour the remaining marzipan with black food colouring. Roll out two-thirds of the brown paste thinly and cut into a 20 × 10-cm/8 × 4-in oblong. Cut the oblong into four 2.5-cm/1-in strips, then cut each strip into eight squares, making 32 in all. Knead the trimmings together and reserve. Repeat with the cream moulding paste and leave until almost set.

Roll out and trim two cream and two brown

strips of moulding paste the width and length of each side of the cake, glaze the cake sides, then place alternate strips around the sides. Brush the top of the cake with glaze. Arrange alternate squares of brown and cream moulding paste on top of the cake. Leave to set. Cut out strips of brown and cream moulding paste to trim the top edges of the cake.

Make the chess men from black marzipan and the trimmings of the cream moulding paste. Leave to set, then arrange them on the appropriate squares on top of the cake.

PLAYING CARDS

2-egg quantity lemon Quick Mix Cake mixture (pages 8–9)
1 quantity Fondant Moulding Paste (page 13)
2 tablespoons Apricot Glaze (page 15)
red and black food colourings
red and black food colouring pens

Line and grease a $28 \times 18 \times 3.5$-cm/$11 \times 7 \times 1\frac{1}{2}$-in oblong tin, spoon in the cake mixture and bake in a moderate oven (160 c, 325 f, gas 3) for 25–30 minutes until well risen and firm. Turn out on to a wire rack, remove the paper, and leave to cool. Make the fondant moulding paste.

Cut the cake into four 14×8.5-cm/$5\frac{1}{2} \times 3\frac{1}{2}$-in pieces and trim. Brush the sides and top of each cake with some of the apricot glaze. Cut the moulding paste into four pieces. Roll out each piece large enough to cover each cake, place them over, press in position and trim neatly to fit.

Knead the moulding paste trimmings together. Cut in half and colour one half red and the other black with a few drops of the food colourings. Roll out the red moulding paste and cut out eight hearts and six diamond shapes, using a cutter or template. Knead the trimmings together and re-roll, then cut out eight thin strips. Arrange the hearts and diamonds on two of the cakes and use the thin strips to make a red border around the top and base of each. Secure with some of the apricot glaze. Using the red food-colouring pen, write the numbers '8' or '6' in the top and bottom opposite corners.

Repeat with the black icing, cutting out five clubs and seven spades and eight thin strips. Place in position on the remaining cakes, secured with the remaining glaze. Using the black food-colouring pen, write '5' or '7' in the top and bottom opposite corners.

GOLF COURSE

3-egg quantity Quick Mix Cake mixture (pages 8–9)
1 quantity Butter Cream (page 14)
green, brown and black food colourings
50 g/2 oz desiccated coconut
1 (30-cm/12-in) thin square silver cake board
2 tablespoons light soft brown sugar
20 orange sticks
small piece of red paper
1 sweet cigarette
1 tablespoon plain chocolate dots, melted
5 curl biscuits
75 g/3 oz Marzipan (page 16)

Line and grease a 28 × 18 × 3.5-cm/11 × 7 × 1½-in cake tin. Spoon in the cake mixture and bake in a moderate oven (160 C, 325 F, gas 3) for 40–45 minutes until well risen and firm to the touch. Turn out on to a wire rack, remove the paper, and leave to cool.

Make the butter cream and colour it green. Place the coconut in a polythene bag with a few drops of green food colouring and shake well to colour evenly. Cut a sloping piece of cake out of the front corner as a bunker. Spread the butter cream icing over the cake to cover it completely, spreading the centre evenly. Cut the spare piece of cake into three, cover each with butter cream and arrange around the top of the cake as landscaping.

Place a 10-cm/4-in plain cutter in the centre, then carefully sprinkle the coconut all over the top and sides of the cake, keeping the centre clear. This makes the green. Place the cake on the cake board and sprinkle the sugar over the bunker to cover it evenly. Carefully remove the cutter. Press the orange sticks in position around the outside of the cake for fencing. Cut out a flag shape from the red paper, attach it to the sweet cigarette and position it in the green. Make a hole near the flag with a straw or something slim.

Spread the melted chocolate over the curl biscuits to coat evenly, leave until set, then press into the cake at the back at different angles for tree trunks. Reserving one-third of the quantity, colour the marzipan green with a few drops of green food colouring. Press out irregular round

shapes, fold and press into the tree trunks to represent the leaves. Roll a tiny ball of plain marzipan and place on the green, then divide the remaining marzipan and colour grey and brown with food colouring. Press into different shaped golf clubs (brown marzipan) and a carrying bag (grey marzipan). Leave to set until firm, then place by the green.

TABLE TENNIS BAT

2-egg quantity Chocolate Quick Mix Cake mixture (pages 8–9)
225 g/8 oz Fondant Moulding Paste (page 13)
brown and red food colourings
100 g/4 oz Marzipan (page 16)
2 tablespoons Apricot Glaze (page 15)
1 mini chocolate roll
icing sugar for sprinkling
1 (30-cm/12-in) round silver cake board

Base-line and grease a 20-cm/8-in sandwich tin, spoon in the cake mixture and bake in a moderate

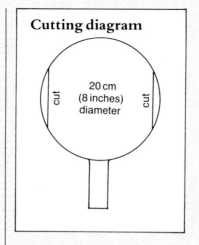

Cutting diagram

20 cm
(8 inches)
diameter

cut · cut

oven (160 c, 325 f, gas 3) for 40–45 minutes or until well risen and firm to the touch. Turn out on to a wire rack to cool.

Make the moulding paste, cut off a piece and make a table tennis ball. Colour the remainder light brown by kneading in a few drops of brown food colouring. Colour the marzipan red with a few drops of red colouring. Trim the edges off each side of the cake, as in the diagram, above. Brush with some of the apricot glaze and place on the cake board. Place the mini roll in position for the handle, putting the cake trimmings underneath to make it level with the cake. Use some apricot glaze to stick them together.

Roll out some of the brown moulding paste on a work surface well sprinkled with icing sugar, making it large enough to cover the bat. Re-roll the trimmings. Carefully lift into position and smooth the icing all over. Trim off the excess icing and neaten the edges. Roll out the marzipan and trim to an 18-cm/7-in round. Mark a pattern on to the surface like a table tennis bat by pressing the coarse side of a grater on to the marzipan. Place the marzipan in position on the bat and mould to the edge. Knead the trimmings together, roll out and cut into a thin strip to place around the base of the cake. Roll the remaining brown icing into a shape to fit the handle and press gently in position. Place the ball on the bat.

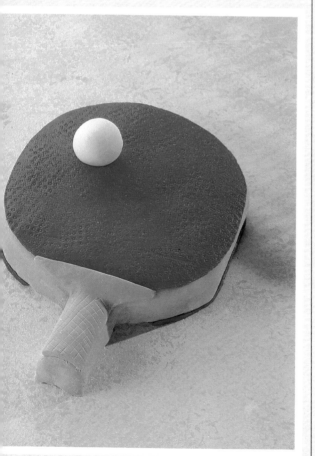

HAPPILY RETIRED

**3-egg quantity Lemon Quick Mix Cake mixture
(pages 8–9)
1 quantity Fondant Moulding Paste (page 13)
yellow and brown food colourings
2 tablespoons Apricot Glaze (page 15)
1 (25-cm/10-in) thin round silver cake board
black food colouring pen**

Line and grease a $26 \times 19 \times 5$-cm/$10\frac{1}{2} \times 7\frac{1}{2} \times 2$-in oblong cake tin, spoon in the cake mixture. Bake in a moderate oven (160 c, 325 F, gas 3) for 50–55 minutes until well risen and firm to the touch. Turn out on to a wire rack, remove the paper, and leave to cool.

Make the fondant moulding paste, then colour two-thirds of it streaky yellow by kneading until coloured in streaks (see small pictures, right), and one third brown with a few drops of the food colourings.

Cut the cake and assemble like a chair, according to the diagram below. Use the cake trimmings to cut out a small cushion and a book. Brush the back and seat pieces with apricot glaze and press together. Place on the cake board. Roll out about one-third of the yellow moulding paste, large enough to cover the seat, front and back of the chair. Place the moulding paste over the cake, press in position and trim to fit. Press the trimmings together.

Roll out another third of the moulding paste and cut out four side arm pieces using the cake shape as a template. Brush the outside of the arm pieces with glaze and press the moulding paste on to each side, then brush the top of the arm pieces with apricot glaze. Press the arm pieces in position. Roll out two long strips of yellow moulding paste to cover the top of each, press in position and trim.

Roll out the brown moulding paste and use to cover the cushion and book case pieces. Use a little more to make a rug and trim it with yellow. Mould the slippers out of scraps of yellow fondant moulding paste. Using the food colouring pen, write the book title on the cover: 'How to Retire Happily', or similar, and assemble the chair and its accessories.

Cutting guide for the cake

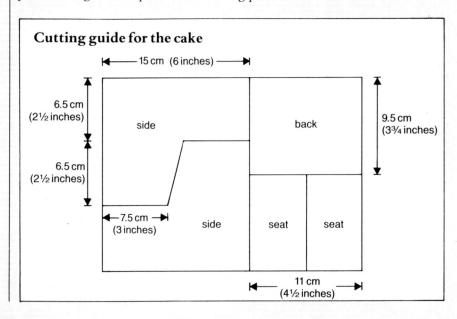

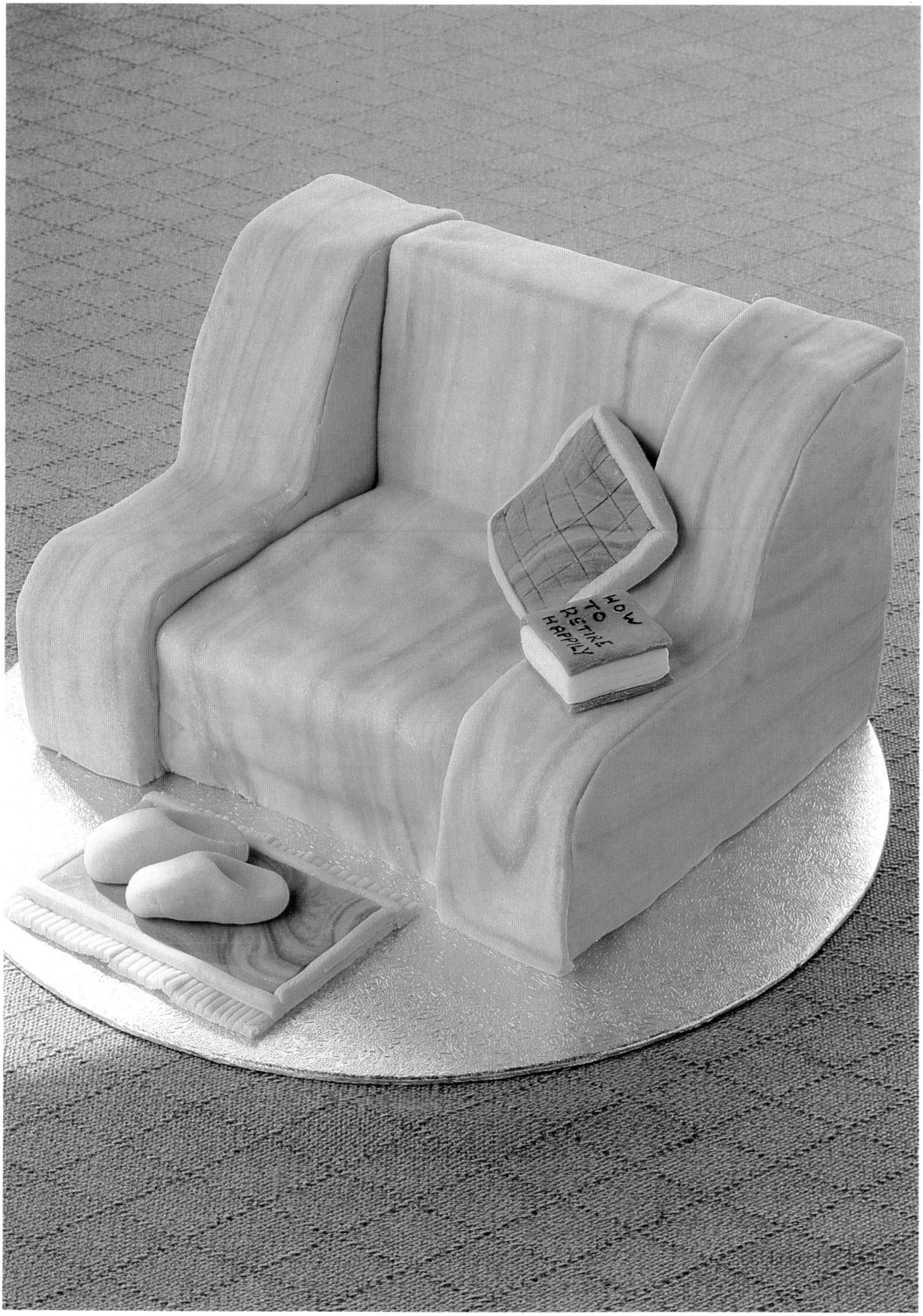
HOW
TO
RETIRE
HAPPILY

Cakes for Christmas

FESTIVE LANTERN

1 egg white, beaten
red, green and yellow food colourings
1½ quantities Biscuit Dough (see Christmas Tree
 Cookies, page 60)
12 yellow and 12 orange thin boiled fruit sweets
1 (18-cm/7-in) square cake board
4 tablespoons Royal Icing (page 18)
50 g/2 oz liquorice comfits
½ metre/½ yard each red and green 2.5/1-in-wide
 ribbons

Make the templates for the lantern following the diagram below. Divide the egg white into three and colour one portion red, one green and one yellow.

Make the biscuit dough. Roll out one quarter of the dough thinly on a baking tray lined with non-stick silicone paper. Using the templates, cut one base and a side piece to make a frame, then place four sweets a little apart in the centre of the frame. Brush the base and frame with alternate stripes of coloured glaze. Bake in a moderate oven (160 c, 325 f, gas 3) for 10–15 minutes until the sweets have melted and filled the centre. Cool on the paper, then remove carefully and transfer to a wire rack.

Repeat to make three more side pieces with four sweets each, four triangular pieces with two sweets each and an open ring for the top. When the pieces are cold, wrap them in cling film until required.

Place the lantern base on the cake board, put the icing into a greaseproof paper piping bag, (see page 16) snip off the end and pipe the edges with icing. Pipe some icing down the long sides of each side piece, then stick on to the base to form a box, gently pressing the sides together. Leave to set for several hours.

Assemble the top of the lantern by piping some icing on two sides of each triangle, but not the base. Using an egg cup as a support, fit the four triangles together, press gently to hold, then leave to set for several hours or overnight.

Pipe a line of icing around the top of the lantern body. Attach the top of the lantern to the body and secure the ring on top with a little icing. Leave to set. Use icing to secure the liquorice comfits down the joins on the top. Thread the ribbons through the ring, if liked.

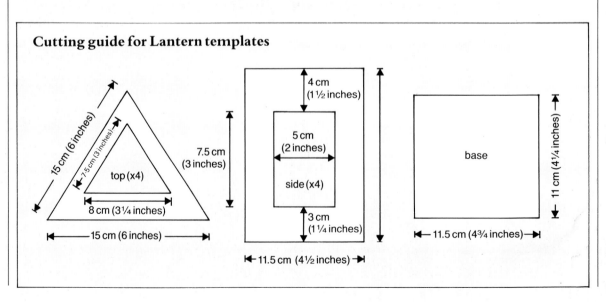

Cutting guide for Lantern templates

15 cm (6 inches)
7.5 cm (3 inches)
top (x4)
8 cm (3¼ inches)
15 cm (6 inches)

4 cm (1½ inches)
7.5 cm (3 inches)
5 cm (2 inches)
side (x4)
3 cm (1¼ inches)
11.5 cm (4½ inches)

base
11 cm (4¼ inches)
11.5 cm (4¾ inches)

CHRISTMAS TREE

6 tablespoons golden syrup
50 g/2 oz margarine
50 g/2 oz light soft brown sugar
350 g/12 oz plain flour
3 teaspoons ground allspice
1 teaspoon bicarbonate of soda
1 teaspoon water
1 (size–3) egg
1 quantity Fondant Moulding Paste (page 13)
green and gold food colourings
2 tablespoons Apricot Glaze (page 15)
2 tablespoons Royal Icing (page 18)
150 g/5 oz milk chocolate balls in foil wrappers
icing sugar to dredge
1 (18-cm/7-in) cake board

Place the syrup, margarine and sugar in a saucepan and heat gently until the margarine has melted. Remove from the heat.

Place the flour and allspice in a bowl. Mix the bicarbonate of soda and water together, then stir into the flour with the egg and the melted margarine mixture. Stir well with a wooden spoon to form a soft dough. Cover and leave for 5 minutes.

Line two baking trays with non-stick silicone paper. Make a Christmas Tree template (see the diagram, below). Roll out a quarter of the dough on one of the lined baking trays. Place the tree shape on top and carefully cut out and remove the excess dough. Bake in a moderate oven (180 C, 350 F, gas 4) for 10–15 minutes until risen and golden brown. Cool on the paper for 10 minutes,

then remove and transfer to a wire rack to cool. Repeat to make four tree cut-outs and a star (using a small star cutter or template). Use the excess dough for gingerbread boys and girls.

Make the fondant moulding paste. Reserve a small piece and tint the remainder of the icing green. Brush each of the tree pieces with apricot glaze. Roll out one eighth of the moulding paste thinly. Place the tree shape on top, glazed side downwards, and cut around the shape (see small picture). Leave to dry. Repeat with the remaining three tree shapes; when the icing has dried, glaze and ice the other sides. Leave to dry.

Spread a thick layer of royal icing in the centre of the board to stand the tree on. Take one tree shape and press into the icing firmly, so that it

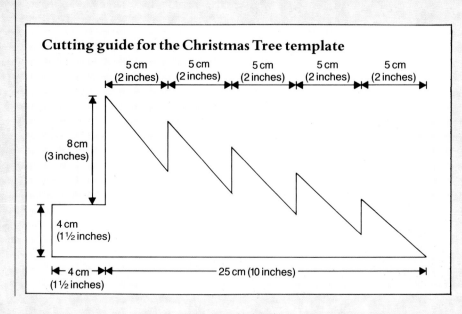

Cutting guide for the Christmas Tree template

5 cm (2 inches) · 5 cm (2 inches) · 5 cm (2 inches) · 5 cm (2 inches) · 5 cm (2 inches)

8 cm (3 inches)

4 cm (1½ inches)

4 cm (1½ inches)   25 cm (10 inches)

stands upright. Spread or pipe the royal icing along each straight edge of each tree shape and press them into the base icing, so that all the straight edges meet in the centre. Press four small pieces of white icing between the tree trunks as supports. Tie a piece of thread underneath the top branches to secure the pieces together until the tree has set.

Cut out a white moulding paste star and attach to the biscuit star with a little apricot glaze. Paint with gold food colouring and leave to set. Pipe a bead of icing on each branch and on the foil-wrapped chocolate balls, then carefully press alternate coloured balls into position. Place the star on top in the same way. Dredge the board with icing sugar.

SANTA IN THE CHIMNEY

3-egg quantity Quick Mix Cake mixture (pages 8–9)
1 quantity Fondant Moulding Paste (page 13)
red, brown, green and blue food colourings
2 tablespoons Apricot Glaze (page 15)
brown food colouring pen
icing sugar to dredge (optional)

Line and grease a 28 × 18 × 3.5-cm/11 × 7 × 1½-in oblong tin and spoon in the cake mixture. Bake in a moderate oven (160 c, 325 f, gas 3) for 40–45 minutes until well risen and firm to the touch. Turn out on to a wire rack, remove the paper, and leave to cool.

Make the fondant moulding paste. Divide into three and colour one portion red and one brown with a few drops of food colouring. Cut the cake according to the diagram right and sandwich the two squares together with apricot glaze. Place on the board and brush the top and sides with glaze.

Roll out the brown moulding paste and trim to a strip as deep as the side of the cake, and 50 cm/20 in long. Carefully fit the paste around

56

Cake cutting diagram

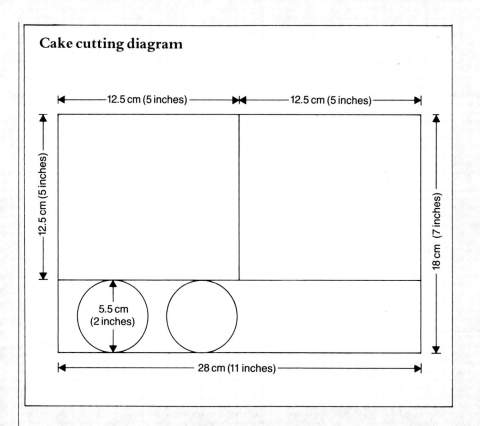

12.5 cm (5 inches) — 12.5 cm (5 inches)

12.5 cm (5 inches)

18 cm (7 inches)

5.5 cm (2 inches)

28 cm (11 inches)

the side of the cake and, using the point of a knife, mark a brick pattern on each side to form a chimney stack. Knead the trimmings together. Roll out the white moulding paste and trim to a 15-cm/6-in square, then leave to set. Knead the trimmings together.

Place the white square in position on top of the chimney stack. Make a 7.5-cm/3-in ring about 2.5 cm/1-in deep from some of the remaining brown moulding paste for the chimney pot and

place in position on the top. To make Santa, use the two cut-out cakes as the head and body. Knead a piece of the brown into some of the white moulding paste to make a flesh colour for the face. Roll out the flesh-coloured moulding paste and use to cover the head. Roll out the red moulding paste and use part to cover the body and part to make a cloak. Cover the body with the red moulding paste and place the head on top, securing with glaze.

Make a beard, hair and eyebrows from some white moulding paste. Colour a piece of white paste blue and make two tiny eyes. Secure the pieces on the cake with a little glaze. Cover the head and body with the cloak and trim the edge with white moulding paste. (Refer to small picture in shaping and assembling Santa.)

Place the Santa into the chimney pot, tucking in the surplus paste. To make the sack, roll out the remaining brown paste and wrap it round a small piece of remaining cake. Draw it together at the top and press. Make a few small shapes from red, blue and green paste for the parcels. Tie the sack with white paste and place on top of the chimney with the parcels in the top of the sack.

NATIVITY SCENE

1 quantity Spicy Dough, see Christmas Tree
 (page 54)
2 tablespoons Royal Icing (page 18)
1 (25-cm/10-in) thin round silver cake board
4 shredded wheat
225 g/8 oz Marzipan (page 16)
blue, green, brown and yellow food colouring
100 g/4 oz Fondant Moulding Paste (page 13)
brown food colouring pen

Make the Spicy Dough according to the instructions (see page 54). Cut out the templates following the diagram below. Roll out the dough thinly
and, using the templates, cut out the roof and back
of the stable, the side pieces and the doors and the
crib pieces. Use a shaped cutter to cut out a star.
Place the pieces on baking trays lined with non-
stick silicone paper. Mark lines with a knife on to
each piece of dough and place a thin strip of dough
across each door piece.

Bake in a moderate oven (180 C, 350 F, gas 4) for
10–15 minutes until well risen and golden brown.
Cool on the paper, then transfer to a wire rack.
Make the royal icing. Assemble the stable by
spreading or piping the edges of each piece with
icing and pressing them together. Secure the
doors with icing. Place on the cake board.

Assemble the crib and secure the pieces with
icing. Crush one shredded wheat and sprinkle
over the floor of the stable. Carefully split the
remaining shredded wheats into half, making six
pieces, and place them in position on the roof.

Cut the marzipan into four pieces. Colour one
piece green, one blue, one brown and one flesh-
coloured (with pink and a dot of brown), using

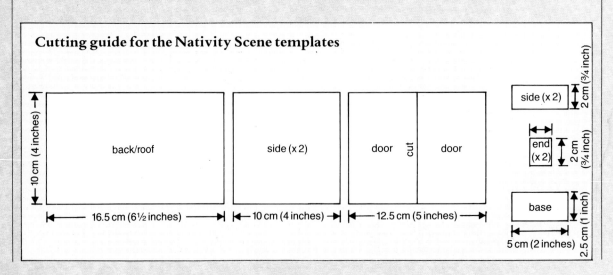

Cutting guide for the Nativity Scene templates

10 cm (4 inches)		
back/roof	side (x 2)	door · cut · door
← 16.5 cm (6½ inches) →	← 10 cm (4 inches) →	← 12.5 cm (5 inches) →

side (x 2) — 2 cm (¾ inch)

end (x 2) — 2 cm (¾ inch)

base — 5 cm (2 inches) / 2.5 cm (1 inch)

the food colourings. Cut off two pieces of fondant moulding paste and colour one piece yellow and the other pale flesh colour. Wrap each in cling film.

To model each of the figures, use white moulding paste to make the baby's cover and the angels' bodies, hands and heads, flesh colour for the baby's head and body and yellow for the halos and wings. Place the pieces together and secure with a little icing. Cut out a yellow moulding paste star to cover the gingerbread star. Place in position on the stable roof.

Make Mary's body out of blue marzipan and the head and hands from flesh-coloured moulding paste. Make some light brown hair and mould the head-dress from white moulding paste. Assemble the figure as above. Using brown marzipan, model Joseph's beard, hair and crook. Make his head and hands from flesh-coloured moulding paste and his body, collar and sleeves from green marzipan (see small picture, top left). Assemble the figure. Make the donkey from the remaining brown and flesh-coloured marzipan. Shape a lamb from white marzipan. Mark all the features in with edible food colouring pens or with tiny pieces of moulding paste or marzipan (see small picture, bottom left). Place the figures around the stable with the baby in the crib.

Small Cakes

CHRISTMAS TREE COOKIES

Biscuit Dough
150 g/5 oz plain flour
25 g/1 oz custard powder
75 g/3 oz caster sugar
75 g/3 oz butter
1 egg (size 3), separated

Decoration
red, green, yellow and orange food colourings
225 g/8 oz thin fruit-flavoured boiled sweets (assorted colours)

Place the flour, custard powder, baking powder and sugar in a mixing bowl. Add the butter, cut into small pieces, and rub in finely with the fingers until the mixture resembles breadcrumbs. Stir in the egg yolk and half of the white and mix with a fork to form a soft dough. Knead on a lightly floured surface until smooth.

Line two baking trays with non-stick silicone paper. Roll out the dough thinly and cut out various shapes using round or square fluted cutters between 5 cm/2 in and 7.5 cm/3 in. in size. Place the shapes a little apart on the prepared baking trays, then cut out the centres with smaller cutters shaped, for example, in hearts, rounds, Christmas trees and bells. Remove the centre shape and place on another baking tray, or knead together to make more full-size shapes and cut out as before.

Divide the remainder of the egg white into four

portions and colour each portion with a few drops of food colouring, so that the egg glazes are red, green, yellow and orange. Using a fine paint brush, paint the frame of each dough shape with different coloured egg glaze. Place a matching fruit sweet in the centre of each shape. If the sweets are too large, cut them in half and place one half in each shape. Make a hole at the top of each shape with a skewer. Paint the centre cut-out pieces if using.

Place the baking trays in a moderate oven (180 c, 350 f, gas 4) and bake for about 10 minutes, until the sweets have melted and filled the space and the biscuits are set.

Leave the biscuits to cool on the paper, then peel off carefully when completely set. Thread a piece of coloured twine through the holes and tie on to the Christmas tree. The small centre pieces can be packed in a glass jar or pretty box. *Makes 25.*

GOLDFISH CAKES

50 g/2 oz Quick Mix Cake mixture (pages 8–9)
3 tablespoons Apricot Glaze (page 15)
3 tablespoons hundreds and thousands
orange food colouring
175 g/6 oz Marzipan (page 16)
cornflour

Grease 15 boat moulds. Divide the cake mixture between them and bake in a moderate oven (160 c, 325 f, gas 3) for about 15 minutes until well risen and firm to the touch. Turn out at once on to a wire rack to cool.

Brush the underneath of each sponge shape with the apricot glaze and just the pointed end of the flat top. Dip the shapes in hundreds and thousands to coat the glazed area. Knead a few drops of food colouring into the marzipan to colour orange. Roll out very thinly on a lightly cornfloured surface.

Using a 1-cm/$\frac{1}{2}$-in plain nozzle, cut out lots of rounds for the fishes scales, then cut out 15 'V' shapes for the tails and 15 rounds for the eyes. Carefully brush the plain sponge with apricot glaze and place the eyes on the hundreds and thousands and the tails at the opposite ends. Arrange the scales overlapping from tail to head. *Makes 15.*

Top left: Christmas tree cookies; **Top right:** Goldfish cakes; **Bottom:** Chocolate truffle cups

CHOCOLATE TRUFFLE CUPS

100 g/4 oz milk chocolate, melted
100 g/4 oz plain chocolate
40 g/1½ oz unsalted butter
1 tablespoon single cream
1–2 tablespoons dark rum or sherry
6 pistachio nuts, peeled and chopped

Place 18 mini paper cake cases on a baking tray. Place half a teaspoonful of melted milk chocolate into one paper case. Using a small brush, spread the chocolate evenly up the side and over the base of the paper case. Repeat to coat the remaining paper cases, using up all the milk chocolate. Leave in the refrigerator or cool place to set hard.

Place the plain chocolate and butter in a bowl over a saucepan of hot water off the heat, stirring occasionally until melted. Stir in the cream and rum until well blended. Remove from the bowl of hot water and leave to cool, giving an occasional stir, until the mixture peaks softly.

Place the chocolate in a piping bag fitted with a medium star nozzle and pipe a swirl of mixture into each chocolate case. Sprinkle with chopped nuts and leave to set. Carefully peel off the paper cases and arrange on a serving plate. *Makes 15.*

SPONGE DICE

**100 g/4 oz quantity Chocolate Quick Mix Cake
    mixture (pages 8–9)**
225 g/8 oz Fondant Moulding Paste (page 13)
red and green food colourings
225 g/8 oz Marzipan (page 16)
6 tablespoons Apricot Glaze (page 15)
cornflour

Line and grease an 18-cm/7-in square tin, spoon in
the cake mixture and bake in a moderate oven
(160 c, 325 f, gas 3) for 35–40 minutes, until well
risen and firm to the touch. Turn out on to a wire
rack, remove the paper and leave to cool.

Cut off a small piece of the fondant moulding
paste the size of a walnut and reserve. Colour the
remaining moulding paste red with a few drops of
red food colouring. Knead a few drops of green
food colouring into the marzipan until evenly
coloured green.

Trim and cut the cake into 16, 3.5-cm/1½-in
squares and brush evenly with apricot glaze. Roll
out the red moulding paste thinly on a surface
sprinkled with cornflour and cut out 40 3.5-
cm/1½ in squares, re-rolling the trimmings when
necessary. Stick the moulding paste squares on to
the sides and tops of eight cakes, pressing the joins
together. Repeat with the marzipan, cutting out
the squares to cover the remaining eight cakes.

Use the reserved white moulding paste to roll
into tiny dots, and secure one to six dots on each
side of the cakes using a little apricot glaze, to
make 16 dice.

YELLOW CHICKS

2 egg whites
100 g/4 oz caster sugar
yellow food colouring
liquorice food colouring pen
150 ml/¼ pint double or whipping cream
2 teaspoons grated lemon rind
10 large chocolate buttons

Line two baking trays with non-stick silicone
paper. Place the egg whites in a bowl and whisk
until stiff. Gradually whisk in the sugar until the
mixture stands up in peaks. Add a few drops of
food colouring to the meringue to colour it pale
yellow.

Place the mixture in a piping bag fitted with a
1-cm/½-in plain nozzle. Pipe a small round of the
mixture about 2.5 cm/1 in in diameter on to the
baking tray for the body and pull off to the right
to form a wing. Pipe a smaller round above and
pull off to the left for the beak. This makes one
half chick. Pipe another half chick with the wing
to the left and the beak to the right.

Repeat to pipe another 15 left-hand chicks and
15 right-hand chicks. Place in a very cool oven
(110 c, 225 f, gas ¼) and cook for about 2 hours, or
until the meringue chicks lift easily off the paper.

Using a fine paint brush and some yellow
colouring, paint the beak and wing markings on
to each chick. Mark in the eyes with the food
colouring pen. Place the cream and lemon rind in
a bowl and whip until thick. Spread half of the
chicks with most of the cream leaving a small
amount and sandwich together with the matching half. Sit each chick on a chocolate button
secured with a little cream.

ANIMAL BISCUITS

150 g/5 oz plain flour
50 g/2 oz ground rice
75 g/3 oz caster sugar
150 g/5 oz soft margarine
1 teaspoon vanilla essence
1 egg, separated
red, yellow and green food colourings
currants

Place the flour, ground rice, caster sugar, margarine, vanilla essence and egg white into a mixing bowl. Mix together with a wooden spoon until the mixture begins to bind together, then knead it with the fingers until the mixture forms a soft dough. Roll out thinly on a lightly floured

From the left: Yellow chicks; Sponge dice; Animal biscuits

surface. Using different shaped animal cutters, cut out the dough and place the shapes on lightly floured baking trays.

Divide the egg yolk into three portions and colour each portion with a few drops of food colouring so that the egg glazes are red, yellow and green. To decorate the animal shapes, brush on either stripes or dots of different egg glaze colours, or just paint on one plain colour. Make the animals' features with currants.

Place the baking trays in a moderate oven (180 c, 350 f, gas 4) and bake for 10–12 minutes until pale at the edges. Cool for a few minutes, then remove carefully and place on a wire rack to cool. *Makes 25.*

INDEX